THINK
LIKE A BOSS

THINK
LIKE A BOSS

Stop Playing Small and Start Thinking Big

MAGGIE COLETTE

HAY HOUSE

Carlsbad, California • New York City
London • Sydney • New Delhi

Published in the United Kingdom by:
Hay House UK Ltd, 1st Floor, Crawford Corner,
91–93 Baker Street, London W1U 6QQ
Tel: +44 (0)20 3927 7290; www.hayhouse.co.uk

Published in the United States of America by:
Hay House LLC, PO Box 5100, Carlsbad, CA 92018-5100
Tel: (1) 760 431 7695 or (800) 654 5126; www.hayhouse.com

Published in Australia by:
Hay House Australia Publishing Pty Ltd,
18/36 Ralph St, Alexandria NSW 2015
Tel: (61) 2 9669 4299; www.hayhouse.com.au

Published in India by:
Hay House Publishers (India) Pvt Ltd, Muskaan Complex,
Plot No.3, B-2, Vasant Kunj, New Delhi 110 070
Tel: (91) 11 4176 1620; www.hayhouse.co.in

A catalogue record for this book is available from the British Library.

Tradepaper ISBN: 978-1-4019-7947-8
E-book ISBN: 978-1-83782-312-3
Audiobook ISBN: 978-1-83782-311-6

10 9 8 7 6 5 4 3 2 1

Printed in the United States of America

This product uses responsibly sourced papers and/or recycled materials.
For more information, see www.hayhouse.com.

To the person who's ready to stop playing small:

It's never too late to change your
life and go after your dreams!

CONTENTS

PART VI: THE MANIFESTO
LIVE LIKE A BOSS

Contents

A NOTE FROM THE AUTHOR

When I first started the Think Like a Boss movement on Instagram in late 2018, it stemmed from a desire to create a community that I couldn't really find online. A community that could be accessed from all corners of the globe by anyone wanting to believe in themselves. What started as a quote account written on a mobile phone has developed into one of the fastest-growing online motivational communities in the world – a haven for people who want to feel motivated, empowered, and inspired to believe that *they can*. Whether it's applying for college, changing careers, leaving a toxic relationship, starting a business, taking up a new hobby, or passing an exam – there is nothing more empowering than feeling like you can. Because when you do, you're halfway there!

Henry Ford, the founder of Ford Motor Company, famously once said:

> *'Whether you think you can, or you think you can't – you're right.'*

Every day, I'm given a stark reminder of why your mindset matters by messages from my community. From teenagers on the brink of suicide, to parents with children who are struggling. Protecting your mind is everything because it can quite literally save your life.

Throughout this book you will be introduced to concepts, tools, and strategies that will support you to step into the most-empowered version of yourself. A manifesto for living life that will stop you playing small and get you thinking big, living big, and winning big.

You see, you're special – and it's not just me who thinks so. It's a scientific fact. Do you know what the probability of being born is? Scientists have estimated that the probability of a person being born is one in 400 trillion.... Think about that for a minute. The chances of you existing are virtually zero. Yet, I bet if I asked you the question: *Are you moving through life like the walking, talking, miracle that you are, believing that anything is possible, and taking action steps to support you to get where you want to be?* the answer is probably 'no' and if you're anything like I used to be, then you're probably limiting yourself to what you believe is true – which is a false narrative inside your head that needs to change.

As you read this book and start to embody what it means to *Think Like a Boss*, I would love to hear from you! Tag me in your favorite quotes from these pages, or any posts about you taking action inspired by this book and let me know what it means to you to #THINKLIKEABOSS.

It's time to stop playing small, start showing up for yourself, and take up the space that you deserve. Be the miracle in this world that you were born to be and empower your loved ones to do the same!

To your success,

Maggie xx

Who would you be if you stopped playing small?

Seriously...

If you stopped playing small and started thinking big, who would you be and what would be different about your life?

Grab a pen and notepad to write down your answer, or write in the notes section on your phone.

INTRODUCTION

While growing up, we're conditioned to be a certain way. We take on thoughts and beliefs from society, school, and loved ones that aren't ours to begin with, but that somehow get molded into us like Play-Doh. We're told that we're 'too this' or 'too that.' Many of us hear that we're also 'not enough.' We go from youngsters who possess a childlike magic, believing that anything is possible, to adults who doubt and question *everything*.

I was 11 years old the first time I was told that I would never amount to anything – a statement that no child or adult wants to hear. The exact opening line that my school teacher bellowed, as he stood on his chair to emphasize his point, was: 'Why are you all so stupid!??' This wasn't a passing remark either. It was a point he spent over 40 painful minutes making, by screaming at my class, until the bell rang for home time.

For context, it was a rainy Monday afternoon and our last lesson of the day. From the moment that French class began, we knew it would be a memorable one for all the wrong reasons. The straw that broke the camel's back came two minutes into the lesson, when one of my classmates stood up to read a passage from a book.

Apparently, he *wasn't reading it right.* Looking back now, it wouldn't have mattered if William Shakespeare was standing at the front of the classroom reading *Romeo and Juliet.* My teacher was clearly having a very bad day and by the time a group of 30 11-year-olds entered his classroom, he'd reached breaking point.

As soon as the bell rang, I've never witnessed so many kids falling over themselves to get out of one classroom. Running from the lesson, we felt a mixture of emotions – confused, frightened, unconfident, worthless, and above all, stupid. We didn't see that teacher again for eight months.

The official line from the school was that 'he was taking time off' – which was odd in itself because term had only just started. But the truth is, most of us went home in tears that night, leading to a number of complaints from parents. I didn't say a word to my mum and dad – they were stressed enough as it was and I didn't want to add to their woes.

We later found out that our teacher had suffered a nervous breakdown. Despite the best efforts of our friendly replacement teacher, it was too late to repair the damage that teacher had done. French rapidly became the subject that my form hated most, especially when it came to studying for tests and exams. A person of authority screaming for 40 minutes that: *You're thick, you're stupid, you can't do it, you're unintelligent, and you'll never amount to anything* was more than enough time to condition a group of impressionable young children into believing that his words were true.

I'm sure you've probably experienced your own version of this story at some point in your life and while it can be easy to excuse a person's behavior and put it down to a bad day, words can have a lasting and detrimental effect. Especially if you hear them often enough and have no idea how to cancel them out. This is why it's so important to protect your mind, so that you can foster the self-belief you need to set yourself up for success.

In addition to exploring your thoughts, this book will introduce you to a new way of being. A manifesto to follow that will inherently open doorways and will lead you to a new way of *thinking*. For this manifesto to work, you need to open your eyes to how you're navigating daily life. From how you walk to how you talk; from your tone of voice to the energy you give off; and how you address those around you.

Have you ever noticed that when you set your mind on something or vocalize a thought and you proactively start researching it, pathways and opportunities suddenly start to present themselves? It can feel like a fluke at first or like a strange coincidence. But the truth is that what you're seeking has always been available to you. Your mind just wasn't open to it, until now.

The phenomenon that I'm describing here is often referred to as the red car theory. A concept rooted in heightened awareness and selective attention that emphasizes the power of recognizing the opportunities that life has to offer when you focus on what you desire. If I asked you a simple question: 'Have you seen any red cars today?' You may reply saying, 'Probably, but I can't tell you how many.' The reason you would give this response (or a variation of it) is because you weren't consciously looking for red cars, so you can't give a precise answer. If, however, you were given an incentive to look for red cars, such as being paid $100 for every red car you see, and I asked you the question: 'Have you seen any red cars today?' – you would know exactly how many red cars you'd seen because you now have a compelling reason to notice them.

The red car theory isn't about red cars *per se*, it's about how humans perceive the world around them. While it might appear that the number of red cars you see has increased, it hasn't, but your awareness of them has. Opportunities are everywhere, but until you actively seek them, you're oblivious to their existence.

My desire for you in reading this book is that you start embodying your inner boss and live the grandest vision possible for your life. But this can only be achieved when you stop playing small and start thinking and acting differently. Another quote attributed to Henry Ford that I've always loved is:

'If you always do what you've always done,
then you'll always get what you've always got.'

And you, my friend, are ready to do something different and play big, otherwise you wouldn't be reading this book. So without further ado, let's get to it!

PART I

NO MORE EXCUSES

ACT LIKE A BOSS

~~I'm too tired.~~

~~It's not the right time.~~

~~I'll start tomorrow.~~

~~I'm too busy.~~

NO MORE EXCUSES.

Before I encourage you to start making changes in your life, I want you to reflect on how you are living currently – especially when it comes to your actions, and whether or not they line up with your intentions.

How often do you talk yourself out of something or use an excuse to justify a decision?

I bet it's way more often than you think! Whether you're finding reasons not to go to the gym or avoiding a particular task, we rely on excuses *a lot*.

In fact, according to a recent study, the average American makes 2,190 excuses a year and six excuses a day to get out of their plans! Of the 2,000 Americans who took part in a poll, 35 percent made daily excuses to avoid exercising, while 33 percent made daily excuses to avoid healthy eating.[1] In comparison, the average British person makes five excuses a day.[2] Both nationalities most frequently used the excuse: 'I'm too tired.' When it comes to excuses, the activities that we most frequently talk ourselves out of include: practicing self-care, running errands, working out, and eating healthily.

#Real Talk:
What excuses have you been using until now that are holding you back from achieving more?

Now, when we come up with excuses, what we're actually doing (for the most part) is self-sabotaging, or as psychologists term it: self-handicapping. This occurs when you behave in a way that sabotages your chances of success. It's something that we're all guilty of and do way more often than we think. In fact, I would even go as far as saying that many of us could be in the running to win an Olympic gold medal if self-sabotaging was a sport!

So, why do we talk ourselves out of things that could help us grow or that could enhance our prospects in some way? For one simple reason: to protect our ego from getting hurt because we're afraid to fail! This is especially true if we're looking to make a key change in our life – one that could alter life as we know it.

You see, when we step into unfamiliar territory, what we're doing is stepping out of our comfort zone. This is something that our ego questions, because its main role is to keep us safe. We then go on to ask ourselves questions such as: is what we want worth the risk of feeling fear, discomfort, shame, sadness, anger, worry, disappointment, or embarrassment, if we were to put ourselves through something and it didn't work out?

This is where the 'do I or don't I?' battle inside your mind begins and unless you're strong-willed enough to push through your fears and Think Like a Boss, then your comfort zone will win, keeping you stuck. We also find it easier to make up excuses than to commit to a goal, because if you commit to a goal and it doesn't work out, you could be left feeling inadequate.

In this section, we'll explore and debunk the top excuses that hold people back from playing a bigger game and look at what you can do to stop self-sabotaging your success.

EXCUSE #1

I'M TOO OLD

*As long as you're alive, your
dreams haven't expired...*

One obstacle that holds far too many people back from creating a better life for themselves or from pursuing their dreams is the belief that they're too old. When the truth is: age is just a number and as long as you're alive, your dreams haven't yet expired!

Just ask Mr. Fauja Singh, who holds the record for being the world's oldest marathon runner. Fauja was 89 when he took up running after the tragic deaths of his wife and son. He ran his first marathon at the grand age of 90 and credits running with saving his life. Dubbed the Turbaned Tornado, Fauja went on to run marathons all over the world including London, Hong Kong, and Toronto, and achieved a personal best of five hours and 40 minutes, before hanging up his running shoes five weeks before his 102nd birthday in 2013!

Mr. Singh continues to hold the world record for becoming the first and only centurion to run a marathon. Although he no longer races, his story continues to inspire people across the world and serves as an important reminder that it's never too late to take up something new or to follow your dreams.

Another story that brings a smile to my face is of Nola Ochs. Nola was 95 years old when she received a degree from Fort Hays State University in 2007, graduating alongside her granddaughter Alexandra. She then went on to earn her master's degree at 98, making her the oldest person to do so at that time.

Here are some more inspiring stories of people who found success later in life:

- **Oprah Winfrey** was fired from her first job as an evening news reporter because she was 'unfit for television news.' She's now one of the most-beloved TV personalities in the world, has touched the hearts of millions of people, and is a self-made billionaire.

- Actor **Harrison Ford** was a carpenter until the age of 39 when he got his first big acting break, landing the role of Han Solo in *Star Wars* and then going on to star in the *Indiana Jones* franchise.

- **Gladys McGarey**, a holistic physician and co-founder of the American Holistic Medical Association, thought she would never recover when her husband and work partner walked out on her after 46 years of marriage and divorced her at the age of 70. In an interview with the online magazine *Fortune Well*, Gladys said that despite her career success in holistic medicine, she didn't really find her voice until she was 93.[3] She went on to deliver a TEDx Talk at the age of 100 and in

2023 published her book *The Well-Lived Life: A 102-Year-Old Doctor's Six Secrets to Health and Happiness At Every Age.*

- **Arianna Huffington** famously once said 'we can build our dreams at any age.' Founding her first company *The Huffington Post*, at the age of 55, Arianna continued building it well into her 60s. She then founded her second company when she was 66. Arianna is an advocate of taking away the pressure of believing we must achieve it all at 30, 40, or any age for that matter.[4] Her story is a wonderful example of pursuing your dreams later in life and not stopping until you achieve your personal version of success.

- **Samuel L. Jackson** is one of the most-beloved and highest-grossing actors of all time. However, this very nearly wasn't the case, as Jackson was plagued with drug addiction for nearly 20 years before getting clean and winning his big break in *Pulp Fiction* at the age of 45.

- Fashion icon **Vera Wang** was a competitive figure skater, a journalist, and a fashion editor in her early career, but it wasn't until she was 40 years old that she decided to pursue her dream of becoming a fashion designer. She now owns an iconic bridalwear label that has a legion of fans across the world. Vera Wang's story is a great example of someone who hasn't had a linear career path. She also highlights that the career you pursue earlier in life isn't always the one that will amass you success and accomplishment later in life.

- **Colonel Sanders'** recipe for Kentucky Fried Chicken was rejected 1,009 times before anyone accepted it. After years of setbacks and misfortunes, including being fired from multiple jobs, having his motel burn down in a fire, and the devastating effects of the Great Depression and World War II, Colonel Sanders refused to give up and finally realized his dream when he franchised Kentucky Fried Chicken in 1952, aged 62. He then went on to sell the company for $2 million in 1964.

- **Viola Davis** is a Juilliard-trained actor and despite making her Broadway debut in 1996, she didn't really make her mark in film and television until 2008, when she was in her early 40s and landed a role opposite Meryl Streep in the film *Doubt*. Davis received an Oscar nomination for best supporting actress for *Doubt*, followed by a best actress nomination for *The Help*. She then became a household name at 51 years old thanks to her lead role in the TV series *How to Get Away with Murder*. This made Davis the first African-American actress to win an Emmy for outstanding lead actress in a drama series. Davis then won her first Oscar in 2017 (for *Fences*) and is currently the most Oscar-nominated Black actress in history.

TIPS FOR BUSTING EXCUSE #1

- **Remember that age is an asset.** The older you are the more wisdom, experience, and resilience you bring. The stories above are just a small handful of powerful examples that there are plenty of people who have accomplished remarkable things later in life.

- **Reframe your perspective.** You are only ever one mindset shift away from a completely different path. Focus on your capabilities and experience, rather than your age. When I think back to what could have been if I'd begun my entrepreneurial journey much earlier, I remind myself that I wasn't ready then. This is a powerful perspective to have. I'm a big believer in trusting the timing of your life. Everything always unfolds exactly how it's supposed to. It's also no coincidence that you're here reading this book at this exact moment.

- **Your time is now.** You owe it to yourself to Think Big, Live Big, and Win Big, irrespective of your season in life. You're never too old to take action. If you feel like you missed out in the past, accept that it wasn't your time – but it is now.

- **Time is a precious gift.** It's something that we all have but it's often taken for granted. Tomorrow is not guaranteed, which is why it's so important to seize the day.

As the stories in this chapter prove, age is but a number. How old you are shouldn't define whether you do or don't attempt something. We are all on our own timeline and life unfolds at a different pace for us all. You're also never too old to start learning or to try something new and find success. If other people can do it, so can you.

IT'S TOO LATE

Do it before you run out of time...

When people tell themselves the story that 'it's too late,' they're really self-sabotaging for one or more of the following reasons:

- They're afraid of failing.

- They have a negative view of themselves.

- They fear change.

- They fear success.

- They have low self-esteem.

I remember holding on to the belief that I'd left it too late to change careers, two years before I eventually quit the banking industry. I was struggling to comprehend how I could give up a career that I'd spent over a decade hustling in, only to start from scratch doing something new. I was deeply unhappy and despite the long hours, continuous travel, and intense levels of stress that came with my role, I was scared of change. It felt easier to use the excuse that I'd left it too late because I'd already spent a decade working my way up in banking. I was also well liked, good at my job, a great manager, and the most senior female in our global department. Could I really give all of that up?' Eventually, the burnout got so bad that I had to prioritize my health and happiness. And once I did, I never looked back!

Did you know that before becoming a priest, Pope Francis worked as a janitor by day and as a bouncer in a Buenos Aires nightclub by night? Award-winning actress and TV host Whoopi Goldberg was a bricklayer and a funeral makeup artist before finding success in showbusiness and becoming one of the few entertainers to win Emmy, Grammy, Oscar, and Tony awards.

Michael Bloomberg was fired aged 39 from the only full-time job he'd ever had. The day after he was dismissed, he started his own company, based on an idea that nearly everyone thought would fail. Within 15 years, Bloomberg became a billionaire. The truth is, as long as you're still alive, it's never too late.

TIPS FOR BUSTING EXCUSE #2

- **Start now, not tomorrow.** The future isn't a given but today is and while you might have a 'life plan,' you never truly know what's around the corner. All we really have is the present moment, so stop blocking your progress and start, before it really is too late.

- **Seek support.** Don't try to do your journey alone, especially if you're guilty of self-sabotaging. Having encouragement and accountability from friends or family can really help you stay focused and on track. Mentorship can also be a game changer – learning from people who have walked the path before you can shave years off your journey, especially if you work with an experienced mentor.

- **If it's on your mind or it's in your heart then it's your sign to start.** Do what you always think about or wonder 'what if?' over, because this feeling won't go away until you do something about it. Remember, time is precious and waits for no one.

- **Avoid comparing yourself to others.** Nothing good ever comes from comparison. It can also feed into the belief that you've left it too late. Everyone's skills, talents, journey, experiences, and circumstances are unique. Just because someone might be younger or further ahead in their journey, doesn't mean that you've left it too late. According to *Psychology Today*, as much as 10 percent of our thoughts involve comparisons of some kind.[5] While people who regularly compare themselves to others may find motivation to improve, they may also experience feelings of inadequacy, and as the infamous saying goes: comparison is the thief of joy. Instead, channel your energy into focusing on what you are doing and stay in your lane, because there's no competition in that lane.

- **Seek inspiration.** Find examples of people who have already done what you want to do or who have overcome similar challenges or obstacles to you and who have pursued their dreams successfully. This can be a powerful way of affirming why it's not too late.

I DON'T HAVE THE TIME

Time isn't the problem.
It's what you're doing with it that is.

How many times have you been asked to do something and out pop the words: 'I don't have the time.'? Now, I'm not disputing how busy life can get, but we're actually worse at time management than we think.

A few years ago, I used this excuse for everything. Yes, I worked long hours and had a jam-packed schedule, but I was also wasting time on activities that weren't adding anything to my life. If anything, they were taking from it. It also seemed easier to say 'no' than to try and create space in my diary. When I discovered the world of personal development, I started tracking my time. Then I realized how much time I was wasting. It also never occurred to me that maybe I needed to work smarter not harder.

Did you know that the average person loses 26 days per year to wasted time?[6] According to a study, we spend nearly two hours a day doing a whole lot of nothing. That's over 12 hours in one week! The most common time-wasting activities are cited as:

- unnecessary meetings
- being disorganized

- procrastinating
- multi-tasking
- lack of delegation
- scrolling on social media
- being kept on hold on the phone
- waiting in line and sitting in traffic

Probably, the most concerning activity is the amount of time we spend on social media. According to a 2024 study conducted by the research company GWI, the average person spends a whopping two hours and 23 minutes per day on social media platforms![7]

While these activities can feel like a by-product of our environment, the vast majority are not. You can get more hours in your day back simply by being mindful about how you're using your time. One action that I recommend is logging how you spend your time for an entire week. From the moment you wake up to the moment you go to sleep, track what you do. You can either do this manually or you can use an app such as Toggl, TrackingTime, or RescueTime.

You'll be amazed at the number of tweaks you can make to give you back more hours in the day, so that you can intentionally invest your time in things that will bring you more joy, happiness, and personal growth.

Imagine pouring one hour daily (which is less than 5 percent of your day) into yourself for a whole year. Whether it's into your self-care or your growth. Replacing one hour a day of Netflix or social media scrolling for working on your dreams and improving your life in some way will take you far. Remember, we all have 24 hours in a day, but it's what we do with our time that matters.

TIPS FOR BUSTING EXCUSE #3

- **Review the meetings in your diary.** Assess if they really need to happen — if they do, issue an agenda in advance. This will help you keep to time, be productive, and avoid any pointless discussions.

- **Tidy your workspace daily.** Not only will this help you with your productivity and energy, but you'll feel ready to take on your day. Remember, a cluttered life is a cluttered mind.

- **Put your mobile phone in a different room.** When possible, put your phone away while you're working or enable flight safe (or airplane) mode on your device. Without it to hand, you will be less likely to get distracted or pick up your phone and waste time aimlessly scrolling.

- **Avoid the rush hour.** If you commute to work, try to schedule your commute at a time when there is less traffic. Invest the time that you save into filling up your cup or moving the needle forward in a passion project.

- **Schedule social media time into your calendar.** Then set a daily reminder or notification five minutes before your allotted time is due to end. This gives you enough time to wrap up any open conversations online.

EXCUSE #4

WHAT WILL PEOPLE THINK OF ME?

People who matter don't judge and people who judge don't matter.

We live in a world where, unless you have a rock-solid mindset and already feel you are enough from the inside out, how people perceive you will likely feel of vital importance. It shouldn't, of course, but sadly the majority of people look to others for approval and seek validation from other sources. This can hold people back from striving for more.

When I first resigned from my career in banking in 2016, I remember meeting my girlfriends one night after work for drinks. As we toasted to a long overdue catch-up, I broke the news that I'd resigned and was walking away from my decade-long career. It was bold, it was risky, and it was scary, especially as I was earning a six-figure salary and didn't yet have the savings to justify quitting – but I was desperate. The pressure and working conditions had gotten so bad that I couldn't take the stress anymore. My mental health was suffering, my body was starting to give in, and I was regularly collapsing on airplanes. To the outside world I was living the dream, but on the inside, I'd reached my breaking point – physically, mentally, and emotionally.

It had taken me 18 months to pluck up the courage to quit from the last private bank I worked for and it wasn't a decision I took lightly. I also didn't have much of a plan, other than to take six months off to travel around Asia and then start a business on my return.

When I first broke the news that I'd quit my career, my friends thought I was crazy. Then the barrage of questions ensued...

What if you fail?

Aren't you scared?

What if things don't work out?

Have you told your parents?

What did they say?

What about your husband?

Will they keep your job open for you just in case?

Are you having a midlife crisis?

It was bad enough trying to quash my own doubts, never mind dealing with theirs. This was also at a time in my life where I hadn't yet discovered mindset or personal development. Thankfully, I was pretty strong-willed and did my best to brush off their concerns, judgment, and comments. Nevertheless, hearing your biggest fears vocalized to you by your closest friends is never fun and made me seriously consider retracting my resignation. I didn't, of course, but I did cry all the way home that night.

Now, when it comes to other people's judgment, these are the most common thoughts that hold people back:

What will they think of me?

What if they laugh?

What if they think I'm crazy?

What if it doesn't work?

What if they don't support me?

One of my favorite celebrity stories about overcoming other people's judgments is that of singer and actress Lady Gaga. When Lady Gaga was at university, a Facebook group was set up called 'Stefani Germanotta, you'll never be famous.' Thankfully, she didn't let this stop her. If anything, it motivated her even more to go out into the world and make something of herself – and boy, did she do that. After a career spanning more than a decade in the music industry, in 2019, Lady Gaga became the first woman in history to win an Oscar, a Grammy, a BAFTA, and a Golden Globe – all in the same year! How's that for winning like a boss?!

Remember, other people's opinions are not your problem and what people say is a reflection of them, not you. As Deepak Chopra famously once said:

> **'What other people think of you is not
> your business. If you start to make
> that business your business, you will be
> offended for the rest of your life.'**

TIPS FOR BUSTING EXCUSE #4

- **Remember that everyone is different.** We all have different values, beliefs, tastes, standards, experiences, and views. What one person finds acceptable or agrees with can be very different to the next person. Accept it and trust that the right people will support you, and anyone who doesn't just isn't your person.

- **Focus on your own goals and values.** What matters is that you're living your life in a way that's true to you. The more energy you channel into doing things for you, the happier and more fulfilled you'll be. Don't let the fear of what others think stop you from pursuing your goals.

- **Work on your confidence and self-acceptance.** The more secure you feel within yourself, the less you will care what other people think. Nothing good comes from taking actions just to appease others. Take actions that align with you and your values and remember that the only opinion that matters is yours. Check out Part III of this book for tips on how to work on your self-worth.

- **Accept that you can't please everyone.** Nor should you try to. It doesn't matter who you are, what you do, or how much you earn, there will always be someone who doesn't like you — and that's okay because you're not here to be liked by everyone.

- **Challenge your negative thoughts.** When you start to worry about what others will think, ask yourself if there's any evidence to support your fears. The exercises in Part IV of this book will also help you to address your negative thoughts.

- **Start small.** Overcoming your worry of other people's judgment won't happen overnight. But you can help yourself by stepping out of your comfort zone and taking steps to address your fears. Try something small to start with, such as speaking up in a meeting. Little by little, a little becomes a lot and with time, your feelings will start to dissipate.

I DON'T KNOW WHERE TO START

You don't need to know where you're going, the key is just to start.

Everyone starts from ground zero. Everyone. Authors, speakers, Nobel Prize winners, all the people you look to for inspiration, leadership, and guidance start with no experience, no audience, no supporters, and no social media following. They also rarely know where to start when they're attempting to get their idea off the ground. So before you allow the overwhelm to get in the way, please, please remember that.

The key is to just start. It doesn't matter where you start, as long as you take action. Remember the red car theory I spoke about earlier in the book – a concept whereby doorways and opportunities will suddenly start to present themselves, as if from nowhere, when you set an intention and start looking into how to get an idea, a wish, or a desire off the ground. This is exactly what will happen when you start to research your idea. The pieces of your jigsaw will start fitting together, once you take that first step and lay the first piece – your idea – down.

Remember, there's no wrong way to get an idea off the ground.

TIPS FOR BUSTING EXCUSE #5

If I was researching a concept or an idea from scratch, with little to no prior knowledge, then I would take these steps to get started:

- **Log onto a computer or mobile phone and head to Google university,** aka www.google.com. Then simply type in what you're searching for e.g. 'boxing classes for beginners in Brooklyn,' or 'how to self-publish a book,' or 'how to start a business.' Then, start by reading a small handful of the articles or blog posts that show up in your search. Once you've read enough articles, you'll start to notice common themes and action steps emerge.

- **Create a to-do list.** Write down the results of your searches as a to-do list, break them down into small action steps, then sort them in order of priority.

- **Join a community of like-minded people.** If you wish to start a business for example, then join a community for new or aspiring entrepreneurs. You could join an in-person community in your local area, or you could join an online community on a platform like Facebook or Telegram. Being surrounded by people who are embarking on a similar journey to you is not only great for holding you accountable, but it will also make you feel less alone and even more empowered to step up your game — especially when you're surrounded by people who are winning.

- **Buy a course, program, or membership.** If you're serious about learning a new skill or taking up a new hobby, then you can't really bypass this stage, especially if you're looking to monetize it at a later date. Knowledge is power, so the more you can educate yourself now, the better. When I first started my online business, I began by investing in a membership program for entrepreneurs, paying $35.99 per month. This gave me access to an online library of resources and monthly Zoom trainings. I soon realized that I needed a higher level of accountability, so I began investing in group programs and masterminds. At a peak, I was investing upward of $2,500 per month on mentoring. If you don't have this kind of budget – don't panic! There are products and programs at every single price point. The key thing is to do your research and don't invest above your means.

The key to succeeding and becoming good at something is to keep persevering. If you stop and start, then you'll get 'stop and start' results. Remember, life is a marathon not a sprint. Dedicate time every single day to bettering yourself in some way and little by little, a little becomes a lot.

I DON'T HAVE THE MONEY

*Invest in yourself –
it pays the best interest.*

We live in a world now where it's never been easier to consume content. Thanks to the internet, YouTube and Google, we have the option to learn for free! So, if you're using 'I don't have the money' as a reason to keep playing small, then get ready to say 'bye Felicia' to this excuse and start thinking big.

I'm a big believer in investing time, money, and energy into passion projects, hobbies, and side hustles. It really does make a difference when you have an expert or a mentor to keep you on track and hold you accountable. But you don't need money to get started! So, if you're a little hard-up on the finance front, then my invitation is to explore what options are available that don't require you to part with money you don't have.

Let's say that you want to learn a new skill like coding, for example. While some people may have the funds to enroll on a course that teaches you the skills you want to develop, there are also free tutorials online that you can source on platforms like YouTube or by doing a Google search. In fact, as I was writing this sentence, I opened a new Google tab to search for free coding courses and was pleasantly surprised to see a number of e-learning websites offering courses for free or an extremely low investment.

TIPS FOR BUSTING EXCUSE #6

There are many ways to pay for degrees, certifications, diplomas, memberships, and subscriptions. Here are just a few ideas:

- **Grants.** There are lots of government grants and funding options available, but until you start doing your research (remember the red car theory), you won't necessarily know what's available to you, as it's not something that's typically well publicized. I remember being hard-pressed for money in my final year at university when a friend of mine, who was struggling financially too, began researching grant options. I remember at the time thinking, *I've already been given the maximum student loan, there's no way that the government will loan me any more money.* Anyway, two weeks later my friend emailed me a link to an application form and I was given a £2,000 grant because the government categorized me as a low-income student. The best bit was that this was a grant, not a loan, which meant that I didn't even need to pay those funds back. I'd say that that's pretty good going for five hours of form filling!

- **Bursaries.** These are monetary awards given by educational institutions or funding authorities to individuals or groups. A bursary is usually awarded to allow a student to attend school, college, or university, who may not be able to do so without it. I've been fortunate to have received a bursary – I was awarded one between the ages of 11 and 18 to attend secondary school and I'm deeply grateful for it. Bursaries are usually offered on the basis of a student's academic abilities, household income, or a combination of both.

- **Tax relief.** This offers a saving, through the tax system, to parents, people on low incomes, people with disabilities, and other groups identified by the government. In effect, it gives certain people extra money. Whilst options and eligibility will differ depending on the country you live in, it's still worth looking into, as every little helps.

- **Loans.** In the same way that you might take out a mortgage to buy a home, you might apply for a loan to get a business idea up and running. Now, I'm in no way advocating that you should do this, I'm merely highlighting that this could be an option. Another option to consider, especially if you have close family members who are financially secure and wish to support you, is taking out an 'interest-free loan' from your parents, sibling, or other relative and agreeing a repayment plan.

- **Negotiating.** I'm a firm advocate of negotiating your way through life, as you'll see throughout this book. Whether it's haggling at a flea market or negotiating a discount on an item of jewelry. If you don't ask, you don't get and the worst someone can say is 'no,' which is no different to the situation you were faced with before trying to negotiate. I've had students ask me for a bonus 1:1 session or extended payment plans and I've always said 'yes,' simply because I admire the fact that they're ballsy enough to ask.

- **Energy exchanges.** This idea got me through my early days of starting a business. I would exchange my time and service with a friend who had a service or skill that I was looking for. For example, a friend would create a logo for me and I would in turn support them with a free coaching session. This can work really well, providing your terms are clear and you're both on the same wavelength.

Hopefully this has given you the confidence and inspiration to let go of this excuse, think BIG and get creative!

IT'S NOT THE RIGHT TIME

There's no wrong time.
If you're waiting for the right time,
you'll be waiting for the rest of your life.

How often have you told yourself the story that 'it's not the right time'?

If you were given $10 for every time you've used this excuse, you'd probably be a millionaire by now – I know I would! Before I became an entrepreneur, I worked in the private banking industry. The hours were long and brutal and the culture was often toxic. Little by little, I could feel my zest for life slipping away, as I found myself longing to exit the career I had built and start a new adventure. But every time I contemplated leaving, I would make excuses for why it wasn't the right time, saying things like:

It's not the right time because I haven't saved enough money yet.

It's not the right time because I'm about to move apartments.

It's not the right time because the market is so uncertain.

It's not the right time because there's an overseas work trip I want to go on.

It's not the right time because I'm waiting for a pay rise.

It took me five years longer than it should have done to walk away from a role that was killing me and it was all because I was scared to take a chance on myself and step into the unknown. Somehow it felt easier to tell myself that it wasn't the right time, and to stay and endure the daily pressures that came with my role, rather than it was to walk away.

The truth is, there is never a wrong time to do something, but we convince ourselves and find reasons like timing to justify our choices, sabotaging our potential for growth in the process. Every day you decide not to do something puts you one day further away from where you want to be. The great news is, it doesn't have to be this way. We all have the same 24 hours in a day and with a little time management and prioritization, you can find a way to make your goals happen if you really want them enough.

TIPS FOR BUSTING EXCUSE #7

- **Confront and challenge yourself** over why you're using this excuse. Is it really true that the time isn't right? What are you afraid of? Is it failure, rejection, or embarrassment? Is it fear of other people's judgment? Once you know what you're afraid of, you can start to address those fears.

- **Set realistic goals.** It can be easy to feel overwhelmed at the prospect of starting something new or different. Especially if it's something that's going to demand more of your time and energy. The key to managing any overwhelm is not to try to do everything all at once. Break down your goals into smaller, more manageable steps. This will make them seem less daunting and more achievable.

- **Create a plan.** Once you know what you want to achieve and how to do it, create a plan of action. This will help you stay focused and motivated. Remember, results don't happen instantaneously. The work you put in now, will pay off in the months and years to come, which is why it's so important to begin sooner rather than later.

- **Take action.** The most important step is to take action. Don't wait for the perfect time because there is never a perfect time. Just start and see where your journey takes you. The sooner you start, the sooner you learn, and the sooner you learn, the quicker you grow.

If you could see into the future with a crystal ball and you knew that 12 months from now you could be in a totally different place and closer to where you want to be, wouldn't you find the time and start taking action today? Or would you keep telling yourself the same old story... and wake up a year from now wishing you'd started today?

WHAT IF I FAIL?

'To learn to succeed, you must first learn to fail.'
MICHAEL JORDAN

While growing up we're conditioned to believe that failure is bad – with a capital B. It starts at school, sitting tests and exams, and then it progresses into adulthood and the workplace. We then associate failure as *the worst thing ever* and, in the process, experience a range of emotions, such as inadequacy, sadness, disappointment, frustration, shame, anxiety, stress, a sense of low self-worth, embarrassment, and anger.

These painful emotions make us want to avoid ever feeling this way again, so we begin to fear failure and play small as a result, sabotaging key areas of our life as adults. A recent survey conducted by Linkagoal and YouGov found that one in three Americans were scared of failing (31 percent) and almost half of the adults surveyed (49 percent) admitted that their fear of failure was the biggest barrier to not achieving their goals.[8]

What's more, the survey also found: 'Millennials are more likely than any other age group to have a fear of failure (40 percent) in comparison with Generation Xers (31 percent) and baby boomers (23 percent).

Women's fear of failure (30 percent) was found to be nearly on par with men's (31 percent).'

As you read this book, I invite you to open your mind to a new way of defining failure – a more empowering one if you like. One where you change the narrative from negative to positive. One where you see failing as an inevitable part of your journey to growth and success. Progress is impossible without challenge, and with challenge comes some of the greatest lessons you will ever learn in life. You have to learn (aka fail) over and over again on your journey to greatness. Arguably, the learnings never stop, especially if you're someone who constantly strives to do better and be better. Everyone has something to teach you and everything has something to teach you. We are all lifelong students in our journey through life.

For example, let's say you want to enter a running competition. If you've never taken up running before, then it's highly unlikely that you're going to win the race on your first attempt – not unless you're naturally gifted at running and are faster than everyone else. But the more you run, the quicker you become and the more you begin to improve on your personal best (PB).

Now, how good would it feel to drop the pressure and expectation on yourself to come first every time you attempt something or enter a race or a competition? What if, instead, you said to yourself: '*Right, I don't have much experience at this yet, but I'll give it a go, give it my best shot, and see what I can learn in the process for next time round.*'? At a guess I'd say that you'd feel relieved because the second you let go of feeling pressured, you start to relax and what you're doing becomes much more enjoyable. You're also likely to think more clearly and perform better because you're less anxious.

If you want to succeed, get comfortable with failing. The more you fail, the more you learn and the more you learn, the more you grow. Your comeback rate, i.e. the speed at which you respond to your failures, is the key to your success. The quicker you can pick yourself up when things don't go to plan, the quicker you'll get to where you want to go.

TIPS FOR BUSTING EXCUSE #8

- **Redefine failure.** The sooner you come up with your own, more empowering interpretation of failure, the quicker you can begin to reprogram how you view it, and the more at ease you'll feel with it.

- **Do a worst-case/best-case scenario analysis.** What's the worst that could happen if things don't work out how you want and what's the best-case scenario? Both scenarios almost always offer better results than you think. As long as no one gets hurt, the worst case is really not that bad and it's never as bad as you make out in your mind.

- **Focus on the lessons learned**. Every time you attempt anything, whether you get the results you want or not, ask yourself the following questions:

  What were my top three learnings from this experience?
  What would I do differently next time? (Providing there are things you'd do differently.)

- **Track your progress.** When you fail, chart your learning, growth, and progress until you reach your end goal.

TOO MANY PEOPLE ARE DOING WHAT I WANT TO DO

Your competition isn't other people.
Your competition is your limiting
thoughts, your bad habits, your fears, your
distractions, and your insecurities.

Not a day goes by where I don't see a variation of some of these messages on social media:

I've left it too late.

There's too much competition.

The market is too saturated.

There are too many people already doing what I want to do.

Ever heard the saying that *thoughts become things?* Sadly, it's true and this statement keeps people playing small because they genuinely believe the hype. However, there aren't enough people in the world thinking big and believing in their capabilities to serve all of those who need your skill, your service, your product, or your solution. Demand is high for skilled people: from dentists and doctors, to school teachers and content creators. So whatever you do, don't buy into the false narrative that too many people are doing what you want to do, because they aren't. The world has never needed more support or more solutions to problems than it does right now.

When I first started my mentoring business back in 2017, I held on to the belief that the coaching industry was saturated. I changed my niche every other month, because I was worried that my business wouldn't survive if I stayed in my chosen niche. It also felt like there was a sea of coaches out there. Why would someone choose me when there were so many other mentors in the online space? There weren't of course, but that seed of doubt was planted, and until I started working with a mindset coach and did the work needed to reprogram my beliefs, it impacted how I showed up in my business and the sales that I made.

I also became obsessed with trying to reinvent the wheel because I thought it's what I needed to do in order to make me stand out. There aren't many new pioneering ideas anymore, so instead of wasting your time trying to come up with the next million-dollar idea, get clear on what lights you up and what you do want to do – the exercises in Part II will help you with this. Remember, if someone, somewhere is already doing what you want to do, and they're making a success out of it, then it's all the evidence you need to show you that the same result or better is possible for you too.

Focus on becoming the best possible version of yourself every day, master your craft, show up for yourself and your career or business, even on the days when you don't feel like it, and know that the work you put in now will pay off in the months and years to come.

TIPS FOR BUSTING EXCUSE #9

- **Reframe your perspective** and stop seeing other people as competition. Instead, embrace the mindset that there is more than enough to go around. Lack breeds more lack and abundance is everywhere – especially when you intentionally seek it, as the red car theory shows. Invest your energy into focusing on your unique strengths and how you can bring something different to the table.

- **Focus on your own journey.** Don't get caught up in comparing yourself to others, because nothing good ever comes from comparison. Everyone's journey is different and what makes you unique is that no one else is you and that is your superpower. Stay in your own lane and stay focused on your own goals and progress.

- **Embrace continuous learning.** Knowledge is power. The more you know, the more valuable you become. Stay up-to-date with what's happening in your field, especially in relation to trends. This will help you stand out from the crowd and be one step ahead.

- **Niche down and identify where you can stand out more.** Is there a specific audience that is underserved or overlooked? Perhaps your employer is crying out for staff to become skilled in a particular area. Get laser focused and strategic – invest your energy into becoming good at something and being known as the go-to person for that thing. Tailor your offerings to meet the unique needs of your audience or clients.

- **Network and be strategic about it.** Get in rooms with people who are where you desire to be and start building relationships. The more people you connect with, the more expansive your network becomes, and, as the saying goes, 'Your network is your net worth.'

WHO AM I TO DO THIS?

Trust yourself.
You can do more than you think you can.

Have you ever held back or stopped yourself from doing something because of thoughts such as:

Who am I to do this?

I don't know what I'm doing.

I'm a fraud.

What if they find me out?

Everyone is so much smarter than me.

I'm not worthy of this.

Thoughts like these are surprisingly normal. It's a phenomenon known as imposter syndrome, which occurs when a person doubts their own abilities and accomplishments, despite evidence of their competence. This can lead to feelings of inadequacy, self-doubt, and anxiety, even in the face of positive feedback or success. It can be rare to go through life without feeling like a fraud or an imposter at some stage. And if you're a high achiever, or someone who constantly strives for more, then you'll experience these thoughts more regularly, until you learn how to push through the noise and nip your thoughts in the bud.

According to the website and magazine *Psychology Today,* around one third of young people suffer from imposter syndrome and 70 percent of everyone else is likely to experience it at some point in their lives.[9] Psychologists Pauline Rose Clance and Suzanne Imes, who coined the term in the 1970s, state that imposter syndrome is tied to our identities and sense of self-worth. They also noted three critical attributes to this phenomenon:

1. Thinking that people have an exaggerated view of your abilities
2. The fear of being exposed as a fraud
3. The continuous tendency to downplay your achievements

Imposter syndrome typically rears its ugly head when we decide to take on new challenges, roles, or responsibilities. Because of the ensuing emotions of worry, fear, and self-doubt, it can be common for sufferers to sabotage their own success and even overcompensate by working twice as hard to prove their worth.

I've lost count of the number of times I've sabotaged my own success by not applying for things or offering my services, because of imposter syndrome and feeling like I was punching above my weight. It all comes back to your sense of self-worth, and until you do the inner work on yourself to feel worthy, then you won't achieve what you're truly capable of accomplishing.

TIPS FOR BUSTING EXCUSE #10

- **Recognize your worth.** You have just as much right as the next person to Think Big, Live Big, and Win Big. Remember, your talents, skills, and experiences are an asset. They make you valuable, so don't be afraid to acknowledge your accomplishments.

- **Challenge any negative self-talk.** Identify and challenge any limiting thoughts and beliefs about yourself. Awareness is key, because once you're aware of what you're thinking, you can proactively take action steps to replace any negative thoughts with positive and more empowering ones. Part IV of this book goes into great detail about this and will be key in supporting you with any limiting beliefs.

- **Seek inspiration from people who have walked your path already.** This will help to motivate you and push past any feelings of self-doubt. When you see that other people have already achieved what you're setting out to do, it reinforces that the same results are possible for you too.

- **Surround yourself with people on the same journey as you.** Join communities or groups where you can connect with people who are also embarking on a similar path or taking up the same hobby or passion project. Having friends, mentors, or professionals to guide, encourage, and support you is priceless and great for accountability.

- **Be mindful of your social media usage.** While there are some incredible benefits to social media, comparison can have negative effects. Following inspirational people may be uplifting, but avoid directly measuring yourself against others. This can lead to feelings of inadequacy and poor self-esteem. Limit your social media scrolling and only follow people who inspire you, motivate you, or educate you.

- **Celebrate your wins.** It can be easy to get swept up in the daily motions of life and move from one goal to the next. Today I invite you to stop, take a minute, and look back on how far you've come. Don't downplay your achievements, instead celebrate them. This is a beautiful way to validate yourself and helps to keep any feelings of imposter syndrome at bay.

YOU NEED NATURAL TALENT TO SUCCEED

You don't need to be naturally gifted or talented at something to be paid for it, or to achieve your definition of success.

Lots of people automatically rule themselves out of trying something new because they don't believe that they're sufficiently smart or talented. Irrespective of what you may have been told when growing up – you don't need to be gifted or talented at something to create a better life for yourself.

But what you do need to have, aside from a want (which we cover in Part II), is something most people don't have: discipline, determination, and the willingness to work at something for long enough before you see results.

In 1993, a study was conducted by Swedish psychologist K. Anders Ericsson in Berlin, who analyzed the practice habits of violin students in childhood, adolescence, and adulthood. All of the participants involved in the study began playing the violin at roughly the same age of five years old. They all had similar practice times; however, as they got older, their times had begun to differ. Then, by the age of 20, the elite performers had averaged more than 10,000 hours of practice each, while the less-able performers had averaged around 4,000 hours.

Now, interestingly, the psychologists didn't see any naturally gifted performers emerge, which surprised them. What they highlighted here is: if natural talent had played a role in violin playing, then it wouldn't have been unreasonable to expect gifted performers to emerge after, say, 5,000 hours, but this wasn't the case.

Ericsson's study concluded that the characteristics that many believe reflect talent are actually, for the most part, the result of deliberate practice, and that practice is the most important factor.[10]

Let's consider another example – learning how to drive a car. When you take the wheel of a car for the first time, it's safe to say you don't know what you're doing. You stall the car more times than you care to admit, and that first lesson makes you feel so frustrated by the end that you question how on earth you're going to pass your test. But with time, consistency, and deliberate practice, driving a car gets easier and easier. The more you practice, the quicker you improve and before long, you're ready to sit and pass your driving test.

While it's true that some people may have a natural aptitude for certain skills, talent isn't the only factor that determines success. So, if you've ever stopped yourself from attempting something because you've held on to the belief that you need to be naturally good at it to succeed, it's time to let go of that story. The more you plug away at something, the more your efforts will compound into results over time.

TIPS FOR BUSTING EXCUSE #11

- **Recognize that talent isn't everything.** While natural talent can give you a head start, it's not the only thing that matters. Hard work, dedication, and perseverance are just as important, if not more so.

- **Focus on your strengths.** Everyone has their own unique strengths and weaknesses. Instead of dwelling on what you struggle with, focus on developing your strengths and talents.

- **Start small and be realistic with your goals.** Don't set yourself up for disappointment from the start by setting the bar too high. Otherwise, you'll feel disheartened before you've even got going. Instead, break down your goals into smaller, more manageable action steps. This will make them seem less daunting and more achievable. Remember, slow and steady wins the race.

- **Be patient.** Success takes time and effort. Don't get discouraged when you don't see results immediately. Success is the result of a compound effect. The work you put in now will pay off at a later date. The key thing is to keep at it and know that eventually, you'll reach your goals.

Remember, anyone can achieve their goals, regardless of their natural talent. The key is having the right mindset and putting in the work.

HOW TO NIP EXCUSES IN THE BUD AND STOP SELF-SABOTAGING

There are two main steps you need to take to stop self-sabotaging:

1. **Recognize and be aware of key behaviors.** Where are you currently not taking action or procrastinating in your life? What excuses are you using that are holding you back? The more aware you become of your behavior and actions (or lack of), the quicker you can do something about them.

2. **Identify the root cause.** Why are you not taking action or making the moves you desire to make? Is it because you feel stressed, overwhelmed, anxious, or fearful? If so, where is this stemming from? Or has someone upset you or said something to make you doubt or question yourself?

At times we self-sabotage because we fear our own success, long before it's even happened. I experienced this a lot in my banking days and it prevented me from putting my name forward for key projects or promotions.

This is a common trait among high achievers, especially if you have a lot on your plate already, as it can cause you to question if you even have the capacity to take on additional responsibilities.

Once you identify what the root cause of your self-sabotaging behavior is, you can start to address it. This might involve having a conversation with someone about delegating or outsourcing some of your current responsibilities to lighten your workload.

Sometimes, when emotions are running high, we may take other people's reactions or behaviors personally and doubt ourselves. For instance, if someone seemed to put you down, it may be that they were merely having a bad day and were too curt. Try to see it from their perspective rather than questioning yourself. Use these tips to help stop self-sabotaging:

1. **Make empowered choices.** When you recognize that you're not thinking big or you're dimming your light, turn around and make a different choice. You have the power to choose differently every second of every day. Choose to do the opposite of the limiting things your ego is telling you and empower yourself. If in doubt, ask yourself this question: 'If I was thinking like a boss right now, what would I do?' Then go and do that thing.

2. **Hold yourself accountable.** You could do this yourself, or seek the support of an accountability buddy, such as a friend or a loved one, or it could be in the form of a mentor, or an experienced colleague. Find someone to hold you accountable and have regular check-ins.

3. **Write down your goals and ambitions on paper.** Don't just do this once, do it as often as you can and take radical responsibility for your actions. See Part II for more about goals.

4. **Track your progress.** This is great for boosting momentum and for looking back to see how far you've come. Set yourself key targets or milestones and make sure to celebrate each time you hit your goals.

5. **Start before you're ready.** As much as you may try to convince yourself you need to wait, you'll never feel ready. The key is to just start, then know and trust that you'll figure things out along the way – the red car theory will help you here.

* * * * * *

There will always be reasons why you shouldn't do something and it will always be comfortable to keep doing what you've always done because your ego's number-one role is to keep you safe.

Don't be that person who talks themselves out of playing a bigger game because it's more comfortable to stay where you are. You're reading this book for a reason and it's not to be in the exact same place one year from now that you're in today. You're here because you're ready to Think Big, Live Big, and Win Big and the only person who can make this happen is you. So, it's time to drop the excuses and let's go!

PART II

INTENTION AND PURPOSE

SET GOALS LIKE A BOSS

Stop ignoring that niggling feeling deep inside of you, telling you that you're destined for more.

Before we explore the subject of what it means to have a want, let's delve into where you are at in relation to your desires right now.

Grab a pen and a journal or notepad and set some time aside (without any distractions) to answer the following questions:

- **Do you want more from your life as you currently know it?** Get vulnerable and go deep here. It's okay to say 'yes,' even if you feel you have more than most.

- **Where in your life are you playing small or not reaching your full potential?** This could be in one or two areas, such as your career or your relationships, or it could even be in all areas of your life. The key here is to be honest with yourself and explore whatever surfaces for you.

- **Why have you been holding back or limiting yourself?** There could be many different reasons here. Fear of other people's judgment could play a role, for example, or perhaps you're scared of your own potential.

- **How could your life change if you gave yourself permission to think big?** Go all out here and dream big. Remember, if it's already been done by someone else, it's proof that the exact same thing is possible for you too...

The purpose of this exercise is to identify where in your life you're currently playing small, as it's something that affects us all and sabotages us. It's not just a one-off thing either. It's a challenge that we face continuously, as we journey through life and evolve as humans. We limit ourselves because of our thoughts and because of what we believe to be true about ourselves, when actually the majority of our thoughts are made up and not the truth. This is why self-awareness is so important, so that we can interrupt any negative self-talk.

NEED OR DESIRE?

It all starts with a *want*. A want for more. And your want either comes from a *place of need* or it comes from a *place of desire*.

The whispers start small and are barely noticeable at first, making them easy to brush off, especially if you lead a comfortable life or if you feel like you have nothing really to complain about. But over time the whispers get louder, until they become so incessant that you have no option but to listen to them.

The Need

Now, if your current situation is less than ideal or you are at the lower end of the income spectrum, then your want is likely to be more compelling, because you may feel a more urgent need to escape your environment, rather than a desire.

I was six years old when my want hit me for the first time from a place of need. I was visiting family in my mum's homeland of Peru, where there were five of us - my mum, my gran, my aunty, my cousin and myself - all squashed into a tiny apartment in the suburbs of Lima.

We had no central heating, very little running water, and we all shared beds.

Our flat was housed in one of those dark and dingy buildings that resembled a cartel-inspired crime drama that you see on Netflix.

One memory from this time that will forever remain ingrained in my psyche, and that I now realize was one of the earliest experiences that instilled my want to create a better life for myself, was bath time. Our apartment was very basic with one bathroom consisting of just a sink and a toilet. Our toilet was one that you manually had to pour water down to flush – this situation was a far cry from the toilets that most people in the Western world are accustomed to... where you just pull a handle and the toilet flushes itself.

When it came to bath time, my mum, my gran, and my aunty would fill a large plastic orange container with cold water and we would take it in turns to wash in it.

At 7 p.m. every evening, Mum would unclothe me and between 7:01 and 7:05 p.m. I would scream my lungs off. To say I hated bath time was an understatement. Being lowered and then dunked into a container of cold water (known today as a cold-water plunge, with far more bougie associations!) felt torturous to a six-year-old, especially if my hair needed washing too. Mum did well to keep it together, given my visible distress, but my cousin, who was 18 months older than me, had no sympathy. It was a reality that hundreds of millions of people living in developing countries faced (and still do). It was also all she knew, as she'd never experienced a hot shower before.

In today's world, people pay good money for their daily cold-water plunge fix... I'm sure you can hazard a guess at how I feel about them! In Latin America in the 1980s, however, being bathed in cold water was a sign of poverty and I for one was categorically unwilling for this to be my reality indefinitely.

I made a promise to my six-year-old self that one day I would make something of myself and be so successful, that I'd be able to afford as many hot showers as I desired and my family would never have to go without.

Now, if you're someone who was born into humble beginnings or you currently live a humble life, this will force you down one of three paths:

1. You work hard because you want to create a better life for yourself.

2. You go off the rails, get into trouble, and find unorthodox means of getting what you want.

3. You settle for what you have or what you've been accustomed to growing up and dim your light because you don't quite believe that you're capable or worthy of more. This may often happen when it's all you've ever known or you're around people who say: *Things like that don't happen to people like us.*

I chose the first path. My childhood lit a fuse in me like no other, so if you have that fuse too, don't ignore it.

Roll with it. Lots of highly successful people come from humble beginnings and go on to create huge success for themselves because of that fuse. Just take Leonardo Del Vecchio – he was one of five children of a widowed mother who struggled to make ends meet. He was eventually sent to an orphanage because his mother couldn't afford to provide for her children. Del Vecchio went to work in a factory making molds for auto parts and eyeglass frames. Then, aged 23, he opened an eyeglass-frame shop that went on to become the world's largest producer and retailer of sunglasses and prescription glasses, Luxottica. When Leonardo Del Vecchio died at the age of 87 in 2022, his net worth was valued at $25 billion according to *Forbes* magazine.[1]

Jan Koum, the co-founder of WhatsApp, was born into poverty. He fled Ukraine with his family and arrived in Mountain View, California, after the collapse of communism in Eastern Europe when he was just 16. Upon arriving in the US, they discovered that Jan's mother had cancer and to make ends meet, sought federal assistance in the form of welfare, food stamps, and government housing. To support his family, Jan went to work in a grocery store. He also went on to learn about computers and cyber security.

In 1997, Jan began working for Yahoo! as an infrastructure engineer, before leaving to launch WhatsApp in 2009. He didn't set out to build a company when he came up with the idea of WhatsApp. Jan just wanted to build a product that allowed people to send messages between mobile phones via the web, regardless of what country they were in. WhatsApp launched in 2009 to critical acclaim and was bought by Facebook, five years later in 2014, for a staggering $19 billion!

Growing up, I didn't ask my parents for much because I was acutely aware of what we did and didn't have, but I did want more. I wanted the same opportunities that kids from higher-income backgrounds had, so I worked for it. I was a self-starter who studied hard from a young age because I needed to.

At the age of 10, I secured a bursary to attend a secondary school that my parents would never have been able to afford otherwise, but I got the grades and coerced them into applying for the bursary. Now, I'd be lying if I didn't admit that I felt like the black sheep at school – a little like an imposter. I'd somehow won one of five golden tickets (as each year only five bursaries were gifted to children from low-income backgrounds) and I felt like I was in my own real-life version of *Charlie and the Chocolate Factory*. I suddenly found myself in a world that I didn't really belong in as if by chance, and it was all because of my burning desire for more. Remember the red car theory: when you actively want and seek more, then opportunities will present themselves as if from nowhere. My bursary was an opportunity, like a gift from God and the universe, that I'd worked for in primary school, and I was damn well sure going to make the most of it.

Between the age of 11 and 18, I was consistently ranked second from bottom in my form, mainly because of the high IQ of pupils in my class. This wasn't ideal and I'd be lying if I said that I didn't feel defeated or suffer from a bruised ego at times, but nonetheless I persevered. I had never been naturally gifted or intelligent, and even though I felt like I had to work 10 times harder than my classmates, I kept going because I knew that with enough work, effort, and determination, I would get there – and I did. I became the first person in my UK family to attend university and went on to secure a good graduate job in London, where I worked in the banking industry for more than 10 years before quitting to become an entrepreneur.

Remember, you don't need to be naturally gifted or intelligent at something to succeed. Hard work, discipline, and determination will get you far. As long as you're willing to put the hours in, you will achieve more than you ever thought possible.

The Desire

Remember I mentioned earlier that the niggling feeling deep inside of you telling you that you're destined for more either stems from a place of need or from a place of desire? Well, you may even experience both at different stages in your life, many times over.

My 'want' from a place of 'desire' first hit me in my late 20s and got progressively louder in my early 30s, until I eventually walked away from a career that I'd accidentally fallen into because it's what I thought success looked like. I'd been working in the banking industry for a decade by this point, mostly in private banking, and I was over it.

Between 2006 and 2017, I witnessed it all in banking: the long hours; the work-hard, play-hard mentality; the cover-ups; the scandals; the blame culture; the drunken Christmas parties; the inappropriate behavior; sexual harassment; racism even. The list goes on and on and on.

I moved banks every two years on average, with the exception of my first role, where I stayed nearly four years. To begin with I thought that it was the bank I was working for that had issues, rather than the industry as a whole. Then it clicked that our salaries were lucrative for a reason, and you either put your head down and got on with it or you got up and walked away. After several years of to-ing and fro-ing, I eventually walked away in January 2017. My stress and anxiety levels were at an all-time high and the burnout had gotten so bad that collapsing on long-haul flights had become my new normal – a reality I wouldn't accept.

In the year leading up to my resignation from my fifth and final banking job, I'd started following an online business coach who was living the laptop lifestyle in Bali. I felt an instant connection to her because I could relate to her story. She'd quit her high-pressure role as a lawyer in the City of London because of burnout and was now living her dream life. Again, the red car theory came into play, because the minute I began searching online for topics such as 'how to start a business,' or 'how to live the laptop lifestyle,' I was inundated with invitations online to register for free challenges and workshops, showing me how to start a side hustle and how to exchange my corporate salary for making even more money by working for myself.

I took this as a sign. The more I started clicking, the more I realized that there was this whole other world available to me that I knew nothing about previously, purely because I hadn't been looking for it until now. Take this as your sign to follow the 'nudge.' Opportunities will always present themselves when you set the intention and start looking for them.

EXPLORING YOUR WANT

Now that you know what it looks like to have a 'want,' you can start thinking about *where* your want stems from. I know you want more and you're ready for change, otherwise you wouldn't be reading this book. To get you started, answer the following questions:

- Is your want coming from a place of need?

- Is your want coming from a place of desire?

- Perhaps it's a bit of both?

Next, get clear on *why* you want more?

Your 'why' will drive you when nothing else does, particularly in those moments where you lose motivation. It also evolves over time. My why at the age of six, was wanting a hot shower. My why at the age of 33 was wanting to escape the stress, anxiety, and burnout that came with a role that I'd begun to hate. My why today is you. I want to empower millions of people across the world to Think Like a Boss and change their life. It doesn't matter who you are, what you do, where you've come from, or how much is in your bank account. The past is the past and it does not dictate, nor is it too late to change your future.

So, why do you want more?

Lastly, let's look at what you actually want. It's okay if you're not sure of this yet and it doesn't need to be a thing, it could be a feeling. Maybe you want to feel a certain way, such as being more calm and peaceful, or have more freedom. We'll explore your want in greater detail later, but for now, I want you to start getting a picture of what you want your life to look like.

A really great way to start identifying this is by reverse engineering and getting clear on how you *don't* want to live your life. Maybe you're tolerating certain activities or behaviors right now that you don't need to anymore. Perhaps you've just become accustomed to a certain way of living and being because it's been your way of life for so long. This needs to change: the sooner you become conscious of what you *don't* want, the sooner you can start working for what you *do* want.

The following exercise may help you with this – try thinking about an area in your life that you want to change and work through each point, writing down on a piece of paper whatever answers come to your mind:

EXERCISE: WHAT IS YOUR WANT RIGHT NOW?

1. What you don't want: the dislike

Ask yourself: What are you currently tolerating in your life that you no longer want?

For example:

- The same salary I was earning five years ago
- Being in a relationship that doesn't light me up
- My increase in body weight

2. What you truthfully want

Ask yourself: What is the desire?

For example:

- To increase my earnings and make more money
- To not be in the relationship anymore and find a partner who adds to my life and makes me feel even more complete
- To love my body, get healthier, and feel good in my clothes again

3. What's the excuse?

Ask yourself: What excuse are you telling yourself about why you're tolerating or doing this behavior or activity?

For example:

- My employer doesn't have the budget to give me a pay rise.
- I've forgotten how to date. What if there's nothing better out there?
- I don't have time to eat healthier food. I'm always on the go. Healthy food is expensive. I don't have time to exercise.

4. What's the truth?

Ask yourself: What's the actual truth?

For example:

- I haven't asked for a pay rise and there are other roles out there that pay more money.

- I can learn how to date. There are over 8 billion people in the world – of course there are many people looking for love and connection.

- I control my life and what I put into my body. Living a healthy lifestyle is a choice and I get to choose.

5. What's the plan to move you closer to what you want?

Ask yourself: What's the new behavior or action plan?

For example:

- Apply for a new role that pays more money, or ask for a pay rise

- End my current relationship and start dating again

- Start meal prepping and make healthy food choices. Start moving my body more. Look at YouTube videos for fitness inspiration.

In point one, you are acknowledging the aspects of your life that you don't want, that don't light you up, or that you're tolerating. This could be a friendship, an activity, a job, or a behavior. In point two, you're declaring what your want or desire is. Don't hold back here and above all be honest with yourself. You can't Think Like a Boss if you're playing small.

Point three is where things get interesting because you're opening your eyes to the excuses you're using that are sabotaging your success. What stories have you been telling yourself that are keeping you stuck or are limiting you? It's time to let them go and take back control – you'll feel much more empowered when you do. Remember, what you believe you are capable of and what you are actually capable of are two entirely different things.

Point four is the game of truth. We make up so many stories inside our heads about what we think is true, but what are the facts? Facts don't lie. They can also add weight to a new way of thinking.

Point five is about your commitment. It's the declaration you're ready to make to yourself about the action you're ready to take – remember, change is nothing without action.

. . . . . .

When you're conscious of your 'want' and you're clear about where it stems from and why you want more, you can start living your life with more intention. The more intentional you are about all aspects of your life, including how you invest your time, your money, and your energy, the better positioned you are to set yourself up to *win*.

Where intention goes, energy flows.

One trait that successful people have in common is living their life with intention and purpose. A person doesn't just become president by accident; nor does a person become fluent in three languages overnight.

To live the grandest possible life for yourself, Think Like a Boss by getting intentional. Studies have shown that people with intention and purpose live longer, experience less stress, have lower levels of depression and anxiety, and have a more robust immune system.[2] This is largely down to the fact that when you have a more compelling reason to wake up every day, you're more likely to take better care of yourself – mentally, physically, emotionally, and spiritually.

In fact, research has found that having a purpose is positively correlated to a person's health and well-being, and may even reduce the risk of premature death. A recent study, published in the *Journal of Preventive Medicine*, monitored a group of people aged over 50 in the US for eight years and found that those with higher levels of purpose lowered their risk of death by 15 percent, compared to people with the lowest sense of purpose, who were found to have a 36.5 percent risk of death from any cause in the same period. The results showed no significant differences in participants' race or ethnicity.[3]

Having a purpose was defined by these researchers as: 'the extent to which people perceive their lives as having a sense of direction and goals.' If we apply this definition to soccer players, as an example, they don't kick a ball for the sake of it. Their goal is to pass the ball around as a team, then shoot and score into their opponents' net and win the game. Matches wouldn't be very exciting if there wasn't a purpose to them and in the same way that soccer players have a purpose in life, so do you.

In this part of the book we'll look at how you can live your life with more intention and purpose and which areas of your life you should prioritize and give the most attention. The more intentional you are about what you do and the actions you take, the happier and more fulfilled you're likely to be.

YOUR LIFE CHECK-IN

To get started, we're going to look at a bird's eye view of your current life and do what I like to call a life check-in. This powerful tool will help you assess where you are, versus where you desire to be. You'll also see very quickly which areas of your life need some TLC. Remember, change is nothing without action!

THE EXERCISE

Over the page you'll find a wheel divided into nine distinct categories, all of which represent a key area in your life.

Review each category and think briefly about what it would mean for you to feel satisfied and fulfilled in all nine areas. Next, on a scale of 1 to 10, circle the number that best represents where you're at currently, with 1 meaning you're extremely dissatisfied and 10 meaning you're extremely satisfied. Think of it as a snapshot of your life in the present moment.

Tip: Don't overthink this exercise. Write the first number that springs to mind and not the number you think it should be.

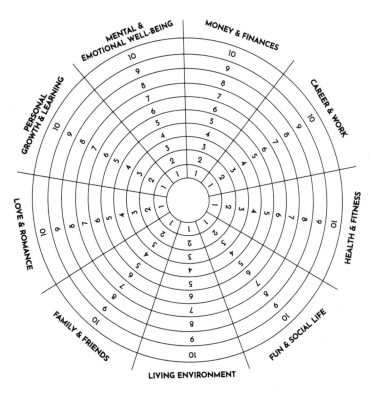

The life check-in wheel

Here are some questions to ask yourself as you work through this exercise:

Money and Finances

What is your relationship with money like and how financially secure do you feel? If you have debt, for example, do you have a plan in place to clear any loans or credit cards? How confident do you feel managing your money? Here, you want to think about your income, savings, debt, financial goals, and overall financial health.

Career and Work

If you work, are you happy with your role and do you feel accomplished in your business or career? Other factors to consider include your overall job satisfaction, job security, opportunities for career development, and whether you have a good work-life balance.

Health and Fitness

What is your physical health and fitness like? Do you have a healthy diet and a good relationship with food? How often are you exercising and moving your body?

Fun and Social Life

Are you creating space in your life for downtime, to go out and have fun? What about hobbies? What are you doing for your own personal enjoyment and to relax and recharge?

Living Environment

What is your living environment like? Think about your home, your neighborhood, and your physical space, including where you spend most of your time. Do you feel that your environment is positively contributing to your well-being?

Family and Friends

What is the quality of your relationships with friends and family? Do you spend enough time with loved ones? Are you part of a community? Do you have people in your life that you can ask for support when you need it?

Love and Romance

How do you feel about your love life? If you have a partner, do they fill your cup and are you in a loving and supportive relationship that contributes to your overall well-being and happiness? If you're single, is it by choice or would you like to meet someone? Are you creating space in your life for romance?

Personal Growth and Learning

Are you setting time aside on a regular basis to work on your personal goals and development? Do you feel content and fulfilled with the progress you're making?

Mental and Emotional Well-Being

How are you feeling? Have you felt stressed or anxious lately? What's taking up most of your headspace right now? How are you sleeping? Is there anything you would like to be different? What did you do today that made you feel good? What can you do for yourself today or in the next few days that would be good for you?

Your Results

Once you've scored each area and jotted your results down on the wheel, I want you to spend some time reflecting and planning. Questions I invite you to reflect on include:

- Are there any surprises for you?

- How do you feel about your life as you look at your results?

- What would a score of 10 look like for you?

- Which three areas would you most like to improve?

- How can you create space to make these changes?

- What help and support do you need from others to improve in these core areas?

- What change *should* you make first? And what change do you *want* to make first?

- If there was one key action you could take that would start bringing everything into balance, what would it be?

- In the past, what behaviors or habits have you stopped doing that could help you improve in these core areas?

Apply Your Results Using Positive Psychology

Before we dive into the core areas of your life that you wish to focus on, I want to introduce you to the PERMAH well-being model. This is a positive psychology well-being framework devised by psychologist Dr. Martin Seligman, containing six core pillars that are proven to be essential to a person's well-being.[4]

For you to score 10/10 in satisfaction, you want each life area on the wheel to touch on these six key pillars:

1. Positive emotions
2. Engagement
3. Relationships
4. Meaning and purpose
5. Accomplishment
6. Health

Positive emotions

According to psychologist and researcher Dr. Barbara Fredrickson, there are 10 positive emotions that most frequently influence people's lives: love, joy, hope, serenity, gratitude, interest, inspiration, pride, awe, and amusement. Fredrickson's broaden-and-build theory asserts that these positive emotions broaden our mind and help us build physical and psychological resources to combat stress. Studies have also found that positive emotions boost our psychological well-being and satisfaction in life by fostering resilience.[5]

Ways to build up positive emotions include spending time with loved ones, surrounding yourself with positive people, putting yourself in situations where you're more likely to feel good, and eliciting positive emotions in others.

Engagement

This refers to being in a state of 'flow' while you're engaged in an activity. Do you ever find yourself losing track of time, especially when you're doing something you love or enjoy? The psychologist Mihaly Csikszentmihalyi's research showed that when you do an activity that you find rewarding, it's more likely to trigger a state of flow within you, as summarized in PositivePsychology.com.[6] Specifically, your brain changes in a way that minimizes distraction, maximizes productivity and performance, and eliminates procrastination.

To get into a state of flow more easily, eliminate anything that distracts you, like your mobile phone – this way you won't find yourself scrolling social media. As Csikszentmihalyi quite rightly put it, 'distraction is the enemy of flow.' Other factors to consider, to help you get into a state of flow, include listening to music, identifying what your most productive time of day is, and doing activities you enjoy.

Relationships

This pillar encompasses our interactions and the level of support we receive from others; whether it's from work colleagues, partners, friends, family, or mentors. As humans, we have an innate desire to feel loved, supported, valued, and connected. Relationships also give our life meaning and purpose. Research has found that:

- People with close social relationships are healthier and more optimistic about the future.[7, 8, 9]

- People experiencing mental ill-health also cite the support of family and friends as being the most important factor in their recovery.[10, 11]

- Friendships formed in the workplace are found to have a positive correlation with performance.[12]

There are many ways to foster better relationships, such as taking an interest in people – when someone feels seen, heard, and special this naturally builds a stronger rapport. Try actively taking the time to nurture existing connections and seek new friendships that will support your overall well-being too.

Meaning and purpose

This refers to having a sense of belonging and serving a purpose that's bigger than you. This could be via your career, your community, your religion, your spiritual beliefs, a social cause, or helping humanity in some way. Our meaning is often guided by our personal values and a desire to feel worthy and valued. Research has found that people who have meaning and purpose in life live longer, have fewer health problems, and have greater life satisfaction.[13]

Ways to cultivate more meaning in your life include investing time into a cause that's important to you, doing activities that you connect with or find rewarding, and using your zone of genius or passion to help others.

Accomplishment

This relates to your achievements. You're more likely to feel accomplished if you're making progress and getting closer and closer to where you want to be. You're also more likely to feel a sense of achievement when you hit your goals and key milestones in your journey. Ways to enhance your sense of accomplishment include setting goals, charting your progress, celebrating your wins, and reflecting on how far you've come.

Health

This encompasses four key components – physical well-being, nutrition, sleep, and restoration. Ways to achieve a healthier lifestyle involve being mindful of and investing time to care for our physical and emotional well-being.

HOW TO IMPROVE KEY AREAS OF YOUR LIFE

Start by asking yourself the question:

When it comes to living my best life in [your chosen area], how can I experience more positive emotions, engagement, support, meaning and purpose, accomplishment, and health in this area of my life?

Let's say you've assigned your career a score of 4 out of 10. The goal is to improve on this and in an ideal world change your score to 10 out of 10. To increase your score, you need to take the right actions. You can only do that when you ask yourself the right questions and use the answers to dictate your actions.

Use the following six-point checklist (which incorporates the six pillars of the positive psychology PERMAH framework) to support you in improving key areas of your life:

1. How can I experience more positive emotions in this area of my life?

2. How can I get into a flow state more often?

3. Do I have good relationships in this area and how can I forge even better relationships?

4. What needs to happen to strengthen my sense of meaning, purpose, and belonging in this area?

5. Am I making progress and do I feel accomplished? What does progress look like to me in this area? What needs to happen to move the needle forward?

6. How can I look after my health and well-being in this area, while allowing my nervous system to feel as calm and supported as possible? What actions need to happen to make this a reality?

Go back to the example of your career. The questions you might want to ask yourself, to increase your career satisfaction score, include:

1. How can I experience more positive emotions in my job? What needs to happen for me to feel more joy, optimism, and happiness at work or in my business?

2. What can I do to get into a flow state more when I'm working?

3. How can my colleagues support me in delivering better results at work to our clients, so that we can improve our client-stakeholder relationships?

4. What can I do to feel more part of the team and like I belong at work?

5. How can I make more progress in my career? Do I need more qualifications or a broader skill set? Should I apply for a new role with better prospects?

6. How can I look after my well-being more, while still doing my job? What actions can I take to help me unwind from work each night, so that I'm not constantly anxious or stressed, and sleep better?

Using this six-point checklist will not only support you to make positive changes in the areas that matter, but you'll feel empowered to take back control and not just go through the motions of everyday life, like so many people do. Remember:

You were born to live, not just to exist.

GOALS AND WHY YOU SHOULD SET THEM

Once you are really clear on the areas of your life that you want to prioritize and why, it's time to set some concrete goals. For clarification: a goal is simply defined as 'the result or achievement toward which effort is directed.'[14]

Goals are important because they give you direction and help you take control of your life. We set goals because we have a desire to expand and grow. So, if you're here to Think Big, Live Big, and Win Big, then get into the habit of goal setting. When you know what you want to achieve, you can make better decisions about how you invest your time, money, and energy. Goals can also help to motivate you, as they give you something to strive for and stay focused. Research has found that setting challenging but achievable goals can also lead to better performance, reinforcing the direct link between setting goals and success.[15]

When you're stepping up your habits game, either to stamp out bad habits or instill new habits, it helps to have a reason (*for more on habits, see Part V, p166*). The more powerful your reason, the more motivated and disciplined you'll be to stick with your goals and build new habits.

So, Why Should You Care?

Apart from the obvious reasons, researchers have found that setting goals also helps people feel more confident, more empowered, and more motivated. However, a recent study published in the *Open Journal of Social Sciences*, conducted by Dr. Michelle Rozen, produced disappointing results. Of the 815 Americans who set at least one goal in January 2023, only 6.5 percent were still pursuing them in June 2023 and 93.5 percent had dropped them. Dr. Rozen's study also found that goal commitment influenced goal setting.[16]

Why You Should Write Your Goals Down

Having goals in your head isn't enough. If you want the best possible chance of winning, you need to go one step further and write them down. In fact, a study conducted by Dr. Gail Matthews at the Dominican University of California on goal setting found that people who write their goals down are more likely to achieve them than those who have no written goals.[17] Making a commitment to a friend about a goal, or sending a friend weekly progress reports, also contributed to success. So writing, commitment, and accountability are all important factors in achieving goals.

Writing down your goals can be beneficial for a number of reasons:

- **It helps you become clear about what you want.** Writing your goals down forces you to think about them in more detail. This then helps you identify what you want to achieve and why.

- **It makes them more real.** Seeing your goals written down makes them more concrete and set in stone. You're then more likely to take action because you believe that they're achievable, which then motivates you further to keep going.

- **It helps you track your progress.** When you have something tangible to work toward, you're more likely to track your progress over time. This can help you stay on track and make tweaks to your actions as needed.

- **It helps you stay motivated to achieve your goals.** It can give you a boost when needed. Referring back to your written goals serves as a powerful reminder of what you're working toward and why.

How to Set Goals

When it comes to setting goals, they should be motivating enough that you want to achieve them, challenging enough that they stretch you – but not so big that they overwhelm you – and meaningful enough that you continue to persevere, particularly in times of adversity. When you set a goal that's too big, you're more likely to fail because you don't necessarily have the space or bandwidth to do the work required, to get the results you desire, in the required timeframe. This is especially true when it comes to forming good habits.

Research on goal-setting theory, which involved reviewing a decade's worth of laboratory and field studies, found that in 90 percent of the studies, individuals performed better when their goals were both specific and challenging, but not too challenging.[18] Research has also discovered that there are a range of health benefits when we write about our life goals, including having a direction and sense of purpose in life,[19] healing through facilitating the release of emotions,[20] identifying internal conflicts and pathways to resolve them, and helping to improve our self-regulation by planning for future events.[21]

As a starting point, think about what goals would feel most meaningful to you right now. What would excite you in terms of achieving and what would help to bring you more joy and excitement in life? Go back to the exercises on pages 60-2. It's much better to start by focusing on areas that are meaningful to you, rather than ones that you feel like you have to address. You're then more likely to accomplish your goals and feel happier and more fulfilled in the process.

My go-to framework for setting goals is the S.M.A.R.T. way, developed by consultant George T. Doran. This method identifies five principles behind setting a goal and all five of these factors should be considered:

S = Specific

M = Measurable

A = Achievable

R = Relevant

T = Time-bound

Here are some tips for writing goals down using the S.M.A.R.T. framework:

Be specific

Don't be vague. Be specific about what you want to achieve and how you plan to do it. For example, instead of writing, 'I want to be healthier,' you could write, 'I want to cut out refined sugars, work out three times every week, and lose 10lbs (4.5kg) in the next six months.'

Make your goals measurable

Make sure you can measure your goals so you can track your progress. For example, instead of writing, 'I want to move my body more,' you could say, 'I want to walk 70,000 steps per week minimum, and do two high-intensity cardio workouts, and one weight-training workout per week for the next six months.'

Set goals that are achievable

Your goals should stretch you, but not to the point where they feel too much. If you set the bar unrealistically high, you're more likely to get discouraged and give up. Start smaller then work upward.

Ensure your goals are relevant

Your goals should be relevant to your life and your values. The more meaningful your goals, the more likely you are to put the effort into achieving them.

Make your goals time-bound

Give yourself a timeline or deadline for each goal. This will help you stay focused and motivated.

Once you've written your goals down, go back and review them regularly. You can then make adjustments as needed, setting new goals every time you either accomplish one, or wish to shift the focus to another area of your life.

GOAL-SETTING EXERCISE

- What did you learn from your life check-in?
- Choose the top three areas you wish to focus on.
- Set three goals for each.

To support you further in this I have created a worksheet, which can be downloaded at www.thinklikeaboss.co/goals.

A Final Note on Goal Setting

Don't give up if things aren't going your way. I will always empower you to Think Like a Boss, but I'm not immune to setbacks and I don't expect you to be either. It's not uncommon to underestimate how long it can take to accomplish a task – especially if you're a high achiever. The key is to keep going. Remember, winners don't quit and quitters don't win!

. . . . . .

When you live your life with intention and purpose, you have a more compelling reason to want to wake up every day simply because your life has direction. Think of it like a compass. When you feel like your life is going somewhere, you feel motivated to plan for the long term and take actions to support the things you value most. Having a purpose helps in every aspect of your life – it may even boost your life span!

So, if you're feeling stuck right now, like so many people are, or you're struggling to see your big vision, please commit to completing the exercises and answering each question, before you move onto the next part of the book.

PART III

SELF-WORTH

VALUE YOURSELF LIKE A BOSS

Your worth is how you see yourself
— not how other people see you.

Read the quote on the opposite page again and let those words sink in for a few minutes.

Your career, your finances, your relationships. Every single aspect of your life is governed by what you believe you deserve. If you believe that you're worthy of a job promotion, then you'll throw your name in the ring for consideration. If you believe that you're worthy of being in a healthy and loving relationship, then you won't tolerate a partner treating you badly.

Your life as you know it is a mirror for how you see yourself and how deserving you believe that you are. Our thoughts, feelings, and behaviors are tied to how we view our worthiness and our value as human beings. The more you value yourself, the better your life will be, because you'll strive for more and stop settling for less.

Sadly, having a lack of self-worth is incredibly common. Even if you have good self-worth in some areas of your life, there may be others where you feel unworthy and constantly settle for the bare minimum. People limit themselves to what they believe is possible for them, because they hold themselves in low regard. People also don't put the effort into creating a better life for themselves because they believe that they don't deserve it. Well, you do deserve it and you are worthy of more. But it's not enough just me saying that – you actually have to believe it.

WHAT IS SELF-WORTH AND WHY IS IT IMPORTANT?

Self-worth is the value and importance you place on yourself, your thoughts, your feelings, and your actions.

A positive sense of self-worth is essential for your overall well-being, as it influences how you treat yourself, how you interact with the world around you, and how you allow others to treat you.

Your beliefs also play a crucial role in shaping your self-worth. Positive beliefs foster a strong sense of self-worth, while negative beliefs undermine it. By understanding the link between beliefs and self-worth, you can take steps to challenge negative thoughts and cultivate a more positive self-image.

What Determines Your Sense of Self-Worth?

According to the self-worth theory, which Martin Covington and Richard Beery share in their 1976 book *Self-Worth and School Learning*, an individual's main priority in life is to find self-acceptance, which is often found through achievement.[1] Their theory identifies four main elements in their self-worth model:

1. Ability

2. Effort

3. Performance

4. Self-worth

The first three elements interact with each other to determine one's level of self-worth. Your ability and effort predictably have a big impact on performance, and all three contribute to the worth and value you place on yourself.

While this theory offers a good model for understanding our experience of self-worth, it places a lot of emphasis on our achievements, which shouldn't be looked at unilaterally.

There are many factors that can contribute to our sense of self-worth and the following are the most common metrics that people typically measure themselves against:

Appearance

Whether it's the color of your hair, the size of your clothes, or the level of attention you receive from others, how we look and what we wear can often impact our sense of self-worth.

Net worth

This refers to your income, financial assets, material possessions: essentially anything that you own.

Your social circle

Who you know and who's in your social circle can impact your bottom line. Some people judge their own value and the value of others by their social status, who's in their social circle, and how influential the people they know are.

What you do/your career

Some people may attribute status to high-earners, such as stockbrokers or bankers, rather than to those who may add value to the community but are paid less, such as nurses or teachers. This is a reflection of an individual's own values as success means different things to different people – but if you feel like others look down on you because your career goals don't match theirs, this may affect how you feel about yourself and impact your self-worth.

Accolades

Awards, rankings, and scores in tests and competitions are often seen as a determining factor in categorizing people as successful.

All of these metrics can negatively impact a person's sense of self-worth because they can lead to feelings of envy, inadequacy, and low self-esteem. Comparing yourself to others using these metrics is also very common and can have a negative impact on how you view yourself. When we compare ourselves to others, we often focus on their strengths and our weaknesses, leading to feelings of inferiority. This can also distract you and cause you to lose sight of your own goals and values.

What Else Impacts a Person's Self-Worth?

There are so many factors that contribute to us viewing ourselves a certain way including:

Personal experiences

Every single experience that you've ever had can contribute to your sense of worth. Life experiences such as wins, losses, successes, failures, relationships, friendships, childhood experiences, and work experiences.

Media and social media

Images we see on billboards, the front cover of magazines, and scrolling on social media offer a certain view of the world and others. A view that isn't always real. Social media platforms, in particular, often showcase idealized versions of people's lives, leading to comparison, feelings of inadequacy, and low self-esteem. Images are also enhanced through filters and editing tools, creating unrealistic standards of beauty, appearance, and how people should live their life.

Your inner critic

Negative self-talk and an overly critical inner voice can undermine your self-worth, as it can reinforce negative beliefs that you have about yourself and your abilities. You're also more likely to dwell on mistakes and failures, which can prevent you from moving forward and learning from your experiences.

Relationships

We often look to feel supported in our relationships – whether they are romantic or platonic. Strong relationships provide emotional support and a sense of belonging, making you feel loved, accepted, appreciated, respected, and understood. Toxic relationships, on the other hand, can erode a person's confidence and shatter their sense of self-worth.

Cultural and societal influences

Cultural norms, societal expectations, and stereotypes can all influence how you may perceive yourself.

Mental health

Certain conditions, such as depression and anxiety, can significantly affect a person's self-worth.

External validation

Relying heavily on external validation, such as praise and recognition, can influence your sense of worth.

EXERCISE: ASSESS YOUR SELF-WORTH

Set some time aside to answer the following questions:

- **What do you want that you currently don't have?** Apply this question to different areas of your life, such as career, finances, relationships.

- **What were the rules in your household regarding worth when you were growing up?** Were you only allowed to have a treat when you worked really hard? Did you always have to earn in order to deserve? Were things taken away from you if you did something wrong?

- **Do you feel deserving?** What reflections come up for you? For example, do you tell yourself that you must work hard to deserve everything that comes your way?

- **What do you think you deserve?** Try to be specific; for example, I deserve to be in a loving relationship, with a partner who is loyal and who treats me with respect, because I am a kind and loving person who gives freely to others.

Let's now look at practical steps and tips for improving your self-worth.

SAY EMPOWERING THINGS TO YOURSELF

*'The most powerful words in the universe
are the ones you say to yourself.'*
MARIE FORLEO

Your inner dialogue, whether it's negative or positive, has a significant impact on your thoughts, your emotions, and your actions. When you speak kindly to yourself it can:

- **Improve your mood and well-being.** Positive self-talk can improve your mood, reduce negative emotions, and promote overall well-being.

- **Increase your confidence and self-esteem.** Empowering self-talk can increase your confidence and self-esteem by reinforcing your worth and capabilities.

- **Enhance motivation and drive.** You can motivate yourself to take action, pursue your goals, and push through any challenges.

- **Increase resilience.** When you talk kindly to yourself and you empower yourself, you are able to cope with challenges and setbacks more effectively.

- **Build stronger connections.** Empowering yourself can improve your relationships and connections because it can make you more empathetic and compassionate toward yourself and others.

LEARN TO ACCEPT COMPLIMENTS

How often do you accept a compliment? Compliments are a form of positive reinforcement that can have a profound impact on your self-esteem – the confidence you have in your abilities and how you value yourself.

PLEASE
TAKE A
COMPLIMENT

I LOVE YOUR ENERGY

YOUR SMILE IS CONTAGIOUS

HOW DID I GET SO LUCKY?

YOU INSPIRE ME

I LOVE YOUR OUTFIT

YOU SHOULD BE PROUD OF YOURSELF

YOU LIGHT UP THE ROOM

YOU'VE MADE MY DAY

When you accept compliments, you are acknowledging your value and your contributions. This can lead to a number of positive outcomes including:

- **Improved relationships.** Accepting compliments can help you build stronger relationships with others. When you are open to receiving compliments, you are showing that you are confident in yourself and that you value the appreciation shown by others. This can lead to more positive and supportive interactions.

- **Increased motivation.** Compliments can serve as a source of motivation. When you receive compliments for your work, contribution, or appearance, it can encourage you to continue showing up at your best and strive for even greater achievements.

- **Improving your mood.** Accepting compliments can boost your mood and make you feel happier. When you focus on the positive things about yourself, it makes you feel good.

- **Helping you develop a more positive self-image.** Hearing positive things about yourself can help you challenge negative thoughts and beliefs.

- **Encouraging you to return compliments to others.** When you accept a compliment graciously, it can create a domino effect, encouraging you to compliment others more.

FOCUS ON YOUR STRENGTHS

They will take you to places your weaknesses can't.

Instead of getting hung up on what you can't do or what you struggle with, focus on what you can do and what you're good at. We all have strengths; the key is to find yours and home in on them. The benefits of focusing on your strengths include:

- **Improved performance.** Focusing on your strengths means that you're more likely to excel in those areas, which can lead to better performance and results.

- **Morale boost.** When you focus on what you're good at, you develop a stronger sense of self-confidence. This can make you more assertive and willing to take on challenges.

- **Reduced stress.** When you focus on your strengths, you are less likely to dwell on your weaknesses, preventing unnecessary stress and anxiety from building up.

- **Greater sense of purpose.** Mastering what you're good at can help you to discover your purpose in life. This can lead to a more fulfilling and meaningful life.

PRACTICE SELF-COMPASSION

Be kind to your mind.

Be kind and understanding toward yourself, even when it feels like you've made a mistake. Forgive yourself and learn from your experiences. When you do this, you're more likely to experience the following:

- **Increased feelings of happiness.** Research highlights that higher levels of self-compassion are associated with heightened 'feelings of optimism, curiosity, and connectedness, as well as lower levels of anxiety, depression, rumination, and fear of failure.'[2]

- **A more regulated nervous system.** When you're kind and supportive toward yourself, you're helping to calm and self-soothe your nervous system. Self-compassion also helps to release oxytocin – a chemical that increases feelings of safety, trust, and calm within your body.[3]

- **Enhanced well-being.** People who are self-compassionate are more likely to experience enhanced psychological well-being and more 'stable feelings of self-worth over time.'[4]

SPEND TIME WITH PEOPLE WHO LIFT YOU UP

Having the right inner circle can be the biggest life upgrade.

Surround yourself with people who empower you and who support you and make you feel good about yourself. Limit your time with negative people or people who drain your energy (*see Protect Your Mind Tip #1, p144*). The benefits of doing so are as follows:

- **Energy is contagious.** When you're surrounded by people who make you feel good, you will instantly benefit from their energy. Energy is contagious (both good and bad). When people exude positive, uplifting, and empowering energy, their energy will transfer onto you.

- **They help to instill the belief that you can.** Interacting with like-minded people who are working on bettering themselves will inspire you to want to do the same. You're also more likely to learn new things and develop new skills because you'll be challenged and inspired by those around you.

- **Feel a greater sense of belonging.** When you're with people who share your values and your beliefs, you're more likely to feel a sense of belonging, and feel part of a community. This can help to boost your self-esteem and your confidence.

- **Improved mental health.** This is because you'll be less likely to feel isolated and alone. You're also more likely to have positive and supportive relationships, which can help to reduce stress and anxiety.

Improving your sense of worth takes time. And it takes effort. But when you appreciate how special you are and how much you can offer the world, not only are you more likely to be happier and more fulfilled, but you're also more likely to stop playing small and start winning big.

Note to self:

Love starts from within.

WHAT IS SELF-LOVE AND WHY IS IT IMPORTANT?

Self-love and self-worth are intrinsically linked and have a significant impact on a person's overall well-being. Whilst self-worth is about how you perceive yourself, self-love is the act of accepting, appreciating, and caring for yourself, regardless of your flaws, appearance, status, or accomplishments.

I'm a strong advocate of self-love, because until you start loving and respecting yourself you can't begin to appreciate the true value that you hold, or the life and the love that you get to welcome, and deserve.

We live in a world where it's normal to put other people's needs above your own. Especially when babies, children, or elderly loved ones are relying on you for their survival. Whilst I'm all for the #PutYourselfFirst movement on Instagram, self-love is *so much more* than a trending hashtag. It's your foundation and internal compass for building confidence, worth, and resilience. When you love yourself, and I mean truly love yourself, you accept the wonderful human that you are, flaws and all. And you treat yourself with the utmost respect, because you know that the one person you're going to spend the whole of your life with is you.

Here, we'll explore how you speak to yourself, the language you use, how you care for yourself, what you do to fill up your cup, how you care for your emotional and spiritual well-being, and how you protect your energy. The thoughts that you think and the actions you take will *always* be reflected back at you. So, if you're not treating yourself with the love and the respect you deserve, then how can you expect anyone else to?

FIND YOURSELF BEFORE YOU FIND SOMEONE ELSE

How often have you jumped from one relationship to the next – without giving yourself a minute to breathe or grieve? Even if you haven't done this, you probably know someone who has and it happens because people are looking for love in the wrong places.

Love is an inside job. It always has been and it always will be. As Whitney Houston famously sang, 'learning to love yourself is the greatest love of all.' So, why is it important to find yourself before jumping into a relationship or partnership?

- **You avoid codependency.** It prevents you becoming overly dependent on a partner for your happiness or sense of self-worth.

- **Enhances your self-awareness.** By getting to know yourself, your values, and your goals, you'll make better informed decisions about who you are, what you desire, and the qualities you look for in a partner.

- **Promotes healthy relationships.** When you're secure in who you are, you're more likely to attract and build healthier and more fulfilling relationships.

- **Personal growth.** Taking the time to discover yourself, allows you to grow as an individual and become a more well-rounded partner.

- **Changes unhealthy patterns.** Understanding yourself can help you break free from unhealthy relationship patterns and make healthier choices.

When you value yourself, others will value you as well. You set the standard of how you are viewed and treated by how you view and treat yourself. So, before you start dating or embark on a new relationship, make sure you know your worth and what you bring to the table.

STOP WAITING FOR A SPECIAL OCCASION: YOU ARE THE SPECIAL OCCASION

How often do you wait to use something that you love? Whether it's a china tea set at Christmas or a sparkly outfit on your birthday – how often do you deny yourself the things that you own and that bring you great pleasure, because you've been taught from a young age that your most-prized possessions should be saved for special occasions?

When I first started thinking about this subject, I underestimated how deeply rooted this way of being is embedded in our psyche. Initially, I restricted the term 'special occasion' to birthdays, anniversaries, weddings, and special celebration days like Christmas. But the more I thought about the topic, the more I realized that we restrict ourselves from using, wearing, or experiencing things that are of value to us all the freaking time. I would even go as far as to say that for many people it's daily, and the worst thing is you probably don't even realize you're doing it, because it's so ingrained into your way of being.

So, what exactly do I mean? Let's take perfume as an example; it's something that many people use daily or very regularly. Now, until a few years ago, my perfume collection looked something like this:

- perfumes I wear to work

- perfumes I wear on a night out

- perfumes I wear on a hot date

They all smelled nice, but they all varied in price and each one made me feel very different. My work perfumes were strictly for work and usually cost somewhere in the region of £20 to £40. My night-out perfumes were more of an investment and were around the £70 to £100 mark; and my hot-date perfumes were upward of £100, with Tom Ford being my go-to. As a caveat, this doesn't have to be about expensive things, as I know everyone's budget is different.

If I was going straight from work on a night out with friends then I'd carry my night-out perfume in my handbag and only spray myself with it when I was leaving work. You'd also never catch me wearing hot-date perfumes for anything other than a hot date, when I want to feel as sexy as possible.

What kind of energy do you think this was giving out?

Not good energy, that's for sure. By picking the cheaper perfume, I was subconsciously saying: *You don't deserve to smell as nice at work, Maggie,* which is ironic given I spent the majority of my time at work and could have benefited from all the extra pick-me-ups I could get!

When you go for the cheaper option and it doesn't make you feel like a million dollars, the same way that something else that you own does, you're sending out a signal to the universe that says you're not enough. When the truth is: *you are,* but until you start doing the work to believe it and show yourself the love that you deserve, then you won't feel it.

You get to feel and smell your BEST
every day, irrespective of what you're
doing or where you're going.

When you do the work and start loving yourself more, you'll start to feel more and more worthy over time. It's only when we step back and look at our behavior, that we can fully start to appreciate how much as a society we deny ourselves, and it's all because we've been programmed to wait for special occasions. Whether it's:

- only lighting your favorite candle at weekends

- only using your favorite skin-care products on a Sunday

- only wearing sparkly outfits at Christmas

- only drinking champagne on your birthday

It's Time to Change the Narrative and Stop Delaying Your Gratification!

How can you cherish your items if they're sitting in the back of your wardrobe in the dark or stored away in your loft getting dusty? You can't. Waiting to use, wear, or experience things can also backfire on you. Not to be morbid but... we all have an expiry date. Which is why it's so important to love yourself, honor yourself, and celebrate yourself.

When you Think Like a Boss you don't wait for a special occasion: *you know that you are the special occasion.* Remember the fact that I shared with you at the beginning of this book about the probability of you being born? If being one in 400 trillion isn't special enough, then I don't know what is.

DRESS HOW YOU WANT TO BE ADDRESSED

This is one of my favorite concepts. I guarantee it'll up-level your life and network in the most magical way possible! Before we dive in, I want to make it clear that I'm not about to ask you to fork out lots of cash on a new wardrobe. In fact, no financial investment is required on your part, unless you're already looking for an excuse to buy new clothes. I also want to highlight that this tip is about so much more than what you wear – it encompasses how you wear something, who you want to embody, and what you desire for yourself.

To begin, I want you to think about the following question:

How do you want people to treat you
when you walk into a room?

What words or sentences spring to mind for you? There's no wrong answer here. The key thing is to be really clear about how you want to be addressed. For example, do you want people to treat you with respect and to take you seriously, or would you rather be invisible to the world and ignored?

Mull it over, and once you're clear on your response, you can start thinking about this next question:

Are you playing the part?

Think of this question a little like role playing. Are you playing the role in the movie that you actually want or are you settling and limiting yourself to what you believe you can get? If, for example, you desire to play a character who's respected and admired, are you looking and acting the part? Or are you showing up as someone who would never be considered for the role, because you're not embodying the character you're trying to portray?

Never forget that you are your personal brand. If you walk into a room and want to command a presence, then how you present yourself matters. From your energy and your confidence, to your appearance and how you hold yourself.

You also never know who you're going to meet or when opportunities may present themselves. Whether you're on a plane, at a bar, or in the restrooms at your favorite restaurant. You just don't know who you're going to cross paths with, which is one of the magical things about life.

How to Dress How You Want to Be Addressed

- **Think about who you want to become** – not who you are right now. Who are you presenting to the world and who do you want to be? The likelihood is that the two are very different – but they should be the same.

Embody the person you want to be, even if you're not there yet.

- **Think about who you want to attract** – irrespective of however unattainable that might feel. You attract people based on how you look, how you dress, and how you carry yourself. If you go to a pub and dress in a sporty way, you're more likely to attract people who love sports. If you go to a bar in a luxury hotel and dress elegantly, you're more likely to attract people who live a glamorous lifestyle, drive expensive cars, and appreciate fashion.

- **You don't need money to dress well** – you can still look good without spending a fortune. In fact, in the first few years of my banking career I was broke. I lived in central London on a salary of £22,000 a year and that had to cover my rent, bills, student-loan repayments, credit-card debt, and travel expenses. By the time my monthly outgoings left my bank account, I had £170 left to spend on food, going out with friends, and on clothes until my next paycheck.

  I was savvy with my money because I had to be. I still looked good and bought myself nice things, but instead of spending £1,000 on a designer blazer, I would spend £30 on a well-cut jacket from a high-street store in the sale, which I'd pair with a £3 vest top from a lower-end shop. Unless you were up close and personal, you would never have known that my vest top cost £3 because I made my outfit work.

If you're not yet where you want to be financially, do what you can with what you've got and be resourceful. Take advantage of sales and shop high-street over designer, unless you find a bargain and you're able to splash out a little more than usual. Accessories can be a great way to up-level your outfits too.

- **Own it** – remember, you have just as much right as the next person to have everything you desire in life. Embody the energy of your higher self and be unapologetic about it. When you own how you look, how you dress, and how you carry yourself, you become a magnet for what you wish to attract. Remember, when you take care of yourself, people take care of you.

IF YOU WOULDN'T SAY IT TO SOMEONE ELSE, DON'T SAY IT TO YOURSELF

One thing that really upsets me is hearing people criticize and talk down to themselves. As humans, we can be mean with a capital M. We also speak negatively about ourselves way more often than we realize. Some of the common disempowering phrases we use are:

I can't do this.

What was I thinking?

Why am I so stupid?

Why does this always happen to me?

What's wrong with me?

I'll never be able to do what they do.

Often, we say these words to ourselves on repeat and unless you're aware of your inner dialogue and take active steps to quell your negative thoughts, then your words can have a detrimental impact and keep you stuck or playing small your entire life.

So, what can you do to silence your inner critic and stop saying things to yourself that you would never dream of saying to other people?

Become More Mindful and Aware of Your Thoughts

The more you open your eyes to the inner workings of your mind, the quicker you can start rewiring your thoughts.

One of my favorite ways to identify and process negative thoughts is through journaling – a powerful self-development tool where you write your thoughts onto paper. In the same way that you may have written your thoughts into a diary as a child or teenager, you do the same as an adult, but in a journal.

The next time you notice Negative Nelly appearing, journal on the following questions and come back to them whenever you need to:

What words or phrases am I saying to myself on repeat that are contributing to me playing small in my life right now?

How is holding on to these words benefiting me?

What are the consequences of repeating negative or limiting words and phrases?

What is the actual truth?

What new thought can I choose for myself today?

To get the most out of journaling, I recommend the following practice:

- Wait until you're home alone or everyone in your household is in bed – that way you won't be disturbed.

- Buy yourself a nice journal, you will be more inclined to write in something you find appealing.

- Create a relaxing environment – consider dimming the lights and lighting a candle, especially if writing at nighttime. You may even wish to scent your environment with a candle or an oil, such as lavender, to enhance relaxation.

- Try to get yourself into a routine where you journal daily, so that it becomes a habit. Maybe begin by writing about your day and what went well for you.

- When you journal, have an open mind and allow yourself to explore the feelings that surface for you. Allow yourself to go deep and be vulnerable – your journal is your safe space. It's also your opportunity for introspection and self-discovery. It's a place where you can explore your emotions and confront any fears.

- You could try using online journal prompts to help you get into the flow. Where a diary typically focuses on recording your events of the day, a journal entry typically delves into the why behind those happenings. Why you feel a certain way and why you reacted the way you did. Journaling is an extremely powerful tool for providing clarity and deeper insights into the self.

Hold Space for Your Inner Critic and Give Him, Her, or Them a Name

Mine is called Mean Maggie, but yours might be called Bitchy Barbara or Devilish Dave. The key thing here is giving your inner critic a voice. They get to be heard, but at the same time you get to make it clear that you aren't going to take what they say as the truth.

Show Yourself Compassion

When you notice that you're being self-critical, forgive yourself for the limiting, negative, or disempowering thought and then replace it with a new, more positive, and more empowering one.

Remember, thoughts become things, and you create your reality every second of every day!

PROTECT YOUR ENERGY: NOT EVERYONE DESERVES ACCESS TO YOU

Everything you do in life requires energy. Whether you're walking across the street, eating breakfast, speaking on the phone, running on a treadmill, going to sleep, or picking up groceries. Every single thing we do as humans requires us to use and exchange energy. The law of physics states that when people use energy, it can only be transformed or transferred. So, when you come into contact with people, there will always be an impact on your energy and this can be good or bad.

Let's say, for example, that you wake up in a bad mood one morning and snap at your partner. If your partner was in a good mood until that point, then unless they are aware of and take actions to protect their energy, their good mood won't last long, because vibrationally a transfer of negative energy has occurred from one person to another. It's highly likely that they'll go from feeling good one minute, to feeling less than great the next, unless they block your energy and protect their space.

So, how can you protect your energy and space in your day-to-day life? Here are some suggestions:

- **Get clear and communicate your working hours.** Make sure people know when you are working – let work colleagues, clients, and family know your hours. Reinforce your working hours with boundaries; for example, you could set up an automated email response highlighting your working hours and how long it will take for emails to be acknowledged. This is a great way of managing expectations and reaffirming your boundaries.

- **Be intentional with your use of technology** and limit your consumption of the news and social media. Decide what time of day you're going to be online and schedule this into your diary. Set a countdown reminder in your phone that notifies you five minutes before your time is up. That way you have advance warning and avoid getting lost in the scroll (*see Protect Your Mind Tips #4 and #5, pp.155 and 159*).

- **Do NOT check your emails or go online at least one hour (but ideally two hours) before bedtime.** Looking at electronic devices can impact your sleep. Ideally, you should be in a theta state – a state of deep relaxation – before going to bed. For more on sleep hygiene, see *How to Practice Good Sleep Hygiene*, p.193.

- **Be mindful of who has close-proximity access to you.** Does anyone in your immediate network drain your energy, such as a work colleague? If so, limit the amount of interaction you have with them and make an excuse to step out of the room when they affect your energy.

- **Intentionally take actions that will support and boost your energy.** Try to stand up and move your body on a regular basis and between meetings. Listen to music, light a candle, change your scenery throughout your day – these actions can do wonders for helping you feel re-energized. Avoid things that drain your energy, such as having back-to-back calls or meetings at work.

- **Be mindful of your triggers.** You might be aware of what these are or you might not be. Sometimes being triggered by someone or something can catch us by surprise. Following people on social media is a common trigger, so if you feel the need to block, mute, or unfollow people – do it. Your emotional well-being comes first. While there are lots of things you can do in the short term to keep triggers at bay, they are usually a sign that something deeper is going on that might need to be healed. Please reach out to an expert who can support you, especially if the same trigger keeps surfacing.

Be mindful of who you allow into your space because your energy impacts everything: how you feel, how you show up, the people you attract, your relationships, your performance. If you find yourself in a situation that you suddenly want to escape, do what you can to remove yourself. It's more than okay to be direct with people. Do what you need to do to protect your energy.

. . . . . .

In this section, I've shared different ways to value yourself more – to improve your self-worth and ideas to promote self-love. Before you jump ahead and start taking action, spend some time reflecting and journaling on the following questions that will expand your sense of self-worth and self-love:

What do you like about yourself?

What do you love about yourself?

How can you show yourself more compassion?

How can you show yourself more forgiveness?

How can you show yourself more love?

What are you holding on to that isn't serving you anymore?

What needs to happen for you to show yourself more love?

While you'll always care deeply for your loved ones, it can be all too easy to put them first and relegate yourself to the bottom of the priority list. This is especially true if you're a renowned people pleaser or have kids, pets, or anyone who needs care.

Let this be your invitation *to not do that* because you can't pour from an empty cup or from one that feels constantly drained. Put yourself first. Romance yourself. Date yourself. Love yourself. Cherish yourself. Clean yourself. Nourish yourself. Treat yourself. Celebrate yourself. Do things for yourself daily and start getting comfortable saying 'no,' especially to things that don't light you up.

Have boundaries and get clear on what you will and won't tolerate. Protect your energy. Surround yourself with people who add to you, *not* take from you. Say 'no' to drama and 'yes' to a calm nervous system.

Remember, love is the greatest force in the universe. Love transmutes energy and heals the world. The more time you invest into loving and appreciating yourself, the more love you can give and receive back from others.

PART IV

UPGRADE
YOUR
MINDSET

THINK LIKE
A BOSS

Take care of your mind.

It's the one place you're in 24/7.

Your number one job is to take care of your mind, because everything flows from there. Whether you're awake or you're asleep, you're in your mind constantly. From the thoughts that you think, to the actions you take, your mind dictates everything.

Before I understood the power of the mind, I had no such thing as boundaries. I watched the news daily and felt depressed every time I turned the TV off. Gossip magazines were my form of escapism, and I naively took everything I read as the gospel truth. Work was hard, the hours were long, and being surrounded by colleagues who were stressed and burned-out also took its toll.

On my 27th birthday, things started to change. I'd come to a bit of a crossroads in my life and the one phrase I couldn't stop repeating to myself was: *there has to be something more out there*. This can't just be it. It was at this point in my life that I began reading self-help books. I needed to believe that there was more available to me, should I choose it.

Not only did these books raise my consciousness, but they also introduced me to two concepts: *thoughts become things* and *what you say and what you think become your reality.*

The concept of *thoughts become things,* which originated from self-help author Bob Proctor, is the idea that positive thoughts and beliefs can lead to positive outcomes, while negative thoughts and beliefs can lead to negative outcomes. When we think positive thoughts, we are more likely to attract positive experiences. Conversely, when we think negative thoughts, we are more likely to attract negative experiences.

The idea that *what you say and what you think become your reality* is similar to the previous concept; however, the focus here is on the power of your words. It suggests that the words we speak and the thoughts we think have a direct impact on our reality. When we speak positive words and think positive thoughts, we are more likely to create a positive reality. Conversely, when we speak negative words and think negative thoughts, we are more likely to create a negative reality.

Before long I was mindful of every single action I took. Negativity was out and empowerment was in. I had one focus and one focus only: to better myself every single day.

I stopped watching the news altogether. I traded gossip magazines for personal development books, and I even cut friends out of my life because I wasn't willing to tolerate their negative attitude anymore. Becoming the happiest and healthiest version of myself was my top priority and if

I wanted to give myself the best possible chance, I needed to start making changes.

**I knew I needed to begin with my mindset,
to overhaul the thoughts and beliefs
that were keeping me playing small.**

You see, we don't just wake up and think good thoughts. We actively have to do the inner work every single day to reprogram our mind and change our limiting beliefs. Oprah Winfrey famously coined the term *we become what we think about*, because your mind rules your life. From our habits and reflexes to our actions and reactions – if you want to win big, start with your mind.

So, what can you do to start thinking big? To welcome any form of change, even on a small scale, you have to start with your thoughts. Did you know that the average person has over 6,000 thoughts per day according to a recent study?[1] Whilst experts have yet to offer any specific estimates around the number of negative thoughts people generally have per day, there's no denying that mental health concerns, such as depression, paranoia, anxiety, and behavioral and emotional disorders, contribute to the number of unwanted thoughts we experience.

Also, 'most people over the age of 30 are said to function in programmed behavior mode', through habits and learned patterns.[2] Learned behavior refers to actions, responses, or reactions that are acquired through experience, education, and observation. An example of a learned behavior is riding a bike. If your programmed behavior isn't supporting you in reaching your goals, then your thoughts and actions need to change, especially if you're serious about living your best life.

THE FOUR PARTS
OF THE MIND

Our mind controls everything. Literally. From the thoughts we think to the actions we take. Everything is ruled by our mind.

The human mind is divided into four parts:

- the unconscious
- the subconscious
- the preconscious
- the conscious

The Unconscious

This is the part of the mind that operates outside of conscious awareness. The unconscious mind encompasses automatic processes such as breathing and digestion, and stores our memories, emotions, and instincts – including everything we've ever thought, felt, or experienced. Think of it like your computer hard drive; nothing is ever forgotten. When we fail to remember certain events or memories, it's because our unconscious has compartmentalized them. If it believes that recalling a certain experience may be a threat to us, then it will deny us access and prevent us from revisiting that memory as a form of protection. You can still access your unconscious mind, it can just take time and may require the support of a clinician.

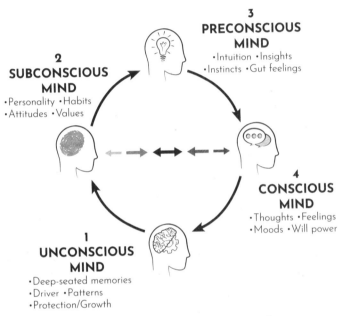

3 PRECONSCIOUS MIND
•Intuition •Insights
•Instincts •Gut feelings

2 SUBCONSCIOUS MIND
•Personality •Habits
•Attitudes •Values

4 CONSCIOUS MIND
•Thoughts •Feelings
•Moods •Will power

1 UNCONSCIOUS MIND
•Deep-seated memories
•Driver •Patterns
•Protection/Growth

The Four Aspects of the Mind (Reach™)[3]

The Subconscious

You could say that the subconscious rules the roost because most of our decisions are made by the subconscious part of our mind. It's where we process thoughts, feelings, and memories without even realizing. Here are some interesting facts about the subconscious mind:

- It's always awake and never sleeps.

- It's habit-based (we'll explore this in detail in the next chapter).

- Your subconscious mind takes everything you say literally. It doesn't know the difference between what's the truth and what's a lie.

- Your subconscious constantly focuses on the present moment, whereas the conscious mind concerns itself with the past and future.

- It can multitask.

The subconscious is also the part of the mind that controls our automatic habits, involuntary functions, and behaviors. Our emotions are also controlled by our subconscious and it has no ability to judge or rationalize. It takes everything we say as the truth, which is why it's vital that we feed it with empowering information.

To change your thoughts and change your life, change your subconscious mind. Later in this chapter I'll share strategies with you on how you can do just that.

The Preconscious

The preconscious (as popularized by Sigmund Freud) is the part of the mind that isn't accessible to conscious awareness but can be accessed with a little effort. It's the part of the mind that exists just below consciousness and stores past memories, thoughts, and feelings that can be easily recalled when needed. For example, you are currently not thinking about your online banking password, but now I've mentioned it, you're able to recall it.

The Conscious

This is the part of the mind that we're aware of at any given moment. It's responsible for our thoughts, feelings, and actions. It's also responsible for our ability to reason, make decisions, and solve problems. The conscious mind is only a small part of the mind. The majority of the mind is unconscious, but both work together to create our reality. The conscious mind is limited in its capacity and is similar to short-term memory.

HOW TO REPROGRAM YOUR MIND

To reprogram your mind, you need to focus on your subconscious because it controls most of your actions.

Let's say you constantly repeat negative phrases such as:

- I'm not clever enough.

- I can't do it.

- Why do I bother?

- It's too hard.

- I'll never make it.

- Good things don't happen to people like me.

Now imagine what these negative thoughts are doing to your confidence, your sense of self-worth, and how this is playing out in your current reality. No wonder you're playing small. Well now it stops. The strategies in this book are here to help you and the best news is that they're all free.

What you believe is what you will attract, every single time. If you believe that life is hard, life will be hard. Remember the red car theory we spoke about earlier? Your brain is constantly looking for pathways and evidence to support your thoughts. In this instance, the experiences that happen throughout your day will reinforce that life is hard, even though there is beauty all around, but you will not see it because you will not be looking for the positive.

The great news is you get to choose what you believe – it will just take time to reprogram your brain. Remember what I said earlier about your mind being like a computer hard drive? You get to upload and process new information all the time. So if you've been a Negative Nelly for far too long or a Grumpy Gerald, then don't panic. You can rewire your thoughts and choose a new thought at any moment. You just need patience and practice to believe the new thought.

FOUR STEPS TO HELP CHANGE YOUR MINDSET

1. Become aware of your current thoughts and beliefs

Pay attention to what you think about yourself, the world, and others. Once you're aware of your thoughts and beliefs you can then start to challenge and change them.

Challenge your negative thoughts. When you catch yourself thinking a negative thought, challenge it. Ask yourself questions such as:

- Is there even any evidence to support this thought?

- Am I really as bad as I think I am?

- Is the world really as hopeless as I think it is?

The answer is almost always 'no.'

2. Replace negative thoughts with positive and empowering statements

Once you've challenged any negative thoughts, replace them with positive ones. It may help you to think about all the good things in life. Some examples of changing negative to positive thoughts are:

- I can't do this to: I can do this or I'm more than capable.

- This is hard to: this gets to be easy.

- Who am I to do this? to: if other people can do this then so can I.

Also think about your strengths, your accomplishments, and positive feedback that you have received from others.

3. Instill new habits

We explore this in great detail in Part V. Your habits can impact your thoughts greatly. To reprogram your mind, you need to develop new habits, which means replacing bad habits with good ones. For example, the next time you're bored, instead of turning on the TV to watch a reality show, read 10 pages of a personal development book.

4. Be patient and above all disciplined

Programming your mind with new beliefs takes time and effort. Don't get discouraged if you don't see results immediately; the key is to keep persevering. One of my favorite reminders when I'm feeling a little impatient is by Usain Bolt, who said:

> *'I trained four years to run nine seconds and people give up when they don't see results in two months.'*

He's right. People want instant results, but life just doesn't work that way. Adopt the mindset of *the work you put in now will be visible six months from now* and keep going until you see results and hit your goals.

Powerful Strategies for Reprogramming Your Mind

As you start to reprogram your mind, try the following:

Using affirmations

These are positive statements that you repeat to yourself on a regular basis. They can change your beliefs, provided you say them regularly enough, and they can also change how you view yourself and your outlook on life.

You can use affirmations to directly challenge a previous negative thought; for example, by replacing *I can't do this*, with *I can do anything I set my mind to.*

When I first discovered the world of mindset and affirmations, I would choose one new belief that I wanted to work on each week and an affirmation to support that belief. For example, *I can do anything I set my mind to.* On day one, which was usually a Monday, I would repeat that affirmation 500 times, usually in quick succession. I would use either a manual clicker to log my repetitions or I would use an app like Tally Counter to click every time I said my affirmation. I'd usually do this activity on my daily walk and it would take me anywhere between 10 and 20 minutes per day to do this practice.

Each day I increased the number of repetitions, so on day two I'd repeat the same affirmation but I'd increase the volume from 500 times to 600 times. Then on day three it would be 750 times and so on. By the end of the week, usually a Sunday, I would repeat my chosen affirmation

2,000 times. It may sound boring and repetitive, but I can honestly say that it worked! It still remains one of my go-to practices to recommend.

Listening to binaural beats

This is an emerging form of sound-wave therapy and involves listening to sound frequencies. I typically use headphones when I'm listening to binaural beats, as I find the practice more effective this way.

Binaural beats present the listener with two different sounds (or beats), each of which operates on a slightly different frequency, but which are perceived by the brain as one single tone. These frequencies help to support the brain in transitioning from a more alert or higher-frequency state into a slower, more relaxed state.

People who listen to binaural beats as part of their daily routine report sleeping better, feeling an improvement in mood, and experiencing increased focus.

A recent study found that binaural beats diminished heart rate variability and it suggests they might be effective in improving your quality of sleep.[4] I'm a firm advocate of this practice and I couldn't recommend it more highly, because of its relaxing effects.

When the beats play at different frequencies, they induce certain states of mind that are more relaxed. It's also been proven that our subconscious mind absorbs information better when we are in a relaxed state.

The reasons for using binaural beats therapy may differ among individuals. I use them for relaxation and for reprogramming my subconscious mind, whereas other people may be seeking support to decrease their anxiety or deepen their level of meditation.

The effects of the binaural beats will depend on their frequency and the corresponding brain wave. Since it takes the brain approximately seven to 10 minutes to be in sync with the audio, you will need to listen to binaural beats for at least 15 to 30 minutes to feel the benefits.

There are binaural beats for so many different things, such as: beats to attract more wealth, better health, improved levels of confidence, healing etc. I was skeptical when I first heard about them, but I quickly became a convert because of how well they work for me. Binaural beats are now a staple part of my bedtime routine and I listen to them as I fall asleep.

If you're keen to give this form of sound healing a try, head to either YouTube or a music app on your phone and search for binaural beats. Then select one that you feel drawn to listen to and plug your headphones in. This is a practice that I've been doing daily for the last few years and it's my favorite form of subconscious reprogramming.

Your mind is your
greatest asset.
Protect it at all costs.

PROTECT YOUR MIND TIP #1

AVOID NEGATIVE PEOPLE

'Stay away from negative people.
They have a problem for every solution.'

ALBERT EINSTEIN

Most people realize that spending time with negative people can have a detrimental impact on your life, but what you might not realize is just how much of an impact they can have.

- **They can bring you down.** Negative people often have a pessimistic outlook on life. You might find that they constantly complain, criticize, or gossip about others. This energy may then rub off on you, making you feel down.

- **They drain your energy.** Negative people can be very draining to be around. They might vent about their problems or regularly seek sympathy, playing the victim rather than the victor. This can leave you feeling exhausted and depleted and may have a knock-on effect on your ability to get your own stuff done. Protect your energy at all costs (*see Self-Love Tip #5, p.122*).

- **They can make you feel bad about yourself.** Negative people often have a lower opinion of themselves and others. They may make snide remarks, put you down, or compare you unfavorably to others. This can damage your self-esteem and make you feel bad about yourself.

- **They can sabotage your goals.** Negative people may not support your goals and may even try to discourage you from pursuing them. They might also have you questioning who you are and why you even think you can achieve them. This can undermine your confidence and impact your motivation levels.

While you can't control other people's behavior, you can control how you respond to them. If you find yourself constantly being dragged down by a Negative Nelly, here are a few actions you can take to protect your energy, which in turn protects your mind:

1. **Set boundaries.** Limit the amount of time you spend with negative people and avoid certain topics of conversation.

2. **Be assertive and stand up for yourself.** Make it clear that you're not available for negativity and state what you will and won't stand for.

3. **Surround yourself with positive people.** Find people who make you feel good and who support your goals. They will help to counteract the effects of negative people.

4. **Prioritize your physical and mental well-being.** This will help you stay strong and resilient in the face of negativity.

Remember, you have the power to choose who you spend your time with.

PROTECT YOUR MIND TIP #2

SET BOUNDARIES

*Having boundaries is the
ultimate form of self-care.*

The price of being a people pleaser can be steep, especially for your mental health. This is why boundaries are so important, but setting them can be easier said than done and some generations find it harder than others.

A recent survey of more than 1,000 Americans conducted by the Thriving Center of Psychology, found that younger generations, notably Gen Z, have the most trouble saying 'no.' The results of the whole survey highlighted that:[5]

- 58 percent of the sample group had trouble saying 'no' to others

- 63 percent considered themselves to be people pleasers

In 2022, 48 percent of the group attended an event that they didn't want to go to, and:

- 72 percent attended events out of guilt or obligation

- 43 percent went to support a friend or family

- 36 percent didn't want to let others down

- 34 percent felt pressured into saying 'yes'

- 13 percent felt pressured to go

In my earlier youth, I said 'yes' to everything: working late nights; taking on more responsibility; attending events. It's like I forgot how to say the word 'no.' I also couldn't face seeing people's disappointment. Nor did I want to miss out on the prospect of being promoted – in case I wasn't seen to be doing *enough*. This led to me feeling tired, unfulfilled, and in a constant state of burnout.

In an interview with CNBC, Harvard-trained psychologist Dr. Debbie Sorensen asserts that people pleasers especially are prone to burnout at work. 'They tend to be very kind, thoughtful people, which makes it much harder for them to set boundaries, not take on too much work, or get emotionally invested in their jobs.'[6] Sound familiar?

Here are the most common signs you might be people pleasing:

- You have a hard time saying 'no' to others even when it goes against your own needs or interests.

- You often find yourself doing things you don't want to do to please others.

- You constantly worry what other people will think of you.

- You're afraid of disappointing others.

- You feel guilty when you don't meet other people's expectations.

- You put others' needs before your own.

- You're constantly seeking approval from others.

- You have a hard time setting boundaries.

- You feel like you're not good enough unless you're pleasing others.

- You're afraid of conflict.

- You have a hard time expressing your own needs or opinions.

When I learned to set boundaries and stop people-pleasing, it changed my game. It was the protector I was crying out for, which I didn't know was available. Once I got clear about what I was and wasn't going to tolerate, I was able to communicate my limits and how people could interact with me. Not only did this give me back some much-needed time and energy, but I noticed a massive improvement in my emotional well-being.

So, why is setting boundaries critical? Here are a few reasons why it might be time to start saying no. It:

- **Reduces stress and anxiety.** Setting boundaries can help with managing expectations and preventing overwhelming situations from occurring. It allows you to prioritize tasks and say 'no' to commitments that might otherwise add unnecessary stress. Boundaries can also be great for minimizing any potential conflict, uncertainty, or resentment from arising.

- **Promotes balance.** Boundaries can help you separate work life from your personal life, minimizing stress in the process. This promotes a healthier work-life balance as it prevents your work from spilling into your personal life.

- **Promotes self-care.** Boundaries enable you to prioritize your physical and mental well-being, which leads you to be happier and healthier.

- **Increases your productivity.** When you have boundaries, you're less likely to get distracted because you're more focused on your tasks at hand. People know when not to disturb you, especially if this has been clearly communicated.

- **Encourages healthy communication.** Setting boundaries encourages open and honest communication, as clear boundaries help to prevent misunderstandings by defining what is and isn't acceptable behavior. When people know what is expected of them, they are less likely to misinterpret or overstep the mark. Boundaries also help to prevent resentment and conflict. When people understand and respect each other's boundaries, they are less likely to feel taken advantage of or disrespected.

- **Prevents burnout and emotional exhaustion.** Setting boundaries can stop you from overcommitting to things that you don't have the capacity to fulfill. This ensures you have sufficient time for rest and self-care, particularly if you work long hours or have a stressful career. Boundaries can also prevent people from draining you emotionally.

- **Protects your energy.** Boundaries help you conserve your mental, physical, and emotional energy. They also enable you to focus and invest your energy into the activities that truly matter to you.

- **Improves relationships.** Healthy boundaries can foster respectful and stronger connections because everyone knows where they stand. They can also reduce the potential for misunderstandings or conflicts.

- **Improves self-respect.** Setting boundaries signals the respect you have for yourself and your worth. It also prevents other people from taking advantage of your kindness or your time.

Remember, having boundaries is an act of self-love. They are crucial for our mental and emotional well-being, while supporting us to lead happier and healthier lives.

What boundaries can you enforce to protect your mind?

BE MINDFUL OF
YOUR SELF-TALK

Your subconscious is always listening.

I'm a firm believer that what you think and what you say is what you attract. So, be careful of your words because the universe *hears everything*. Your words are like spells. We spell words and we also cast spells with our words. Each time you speak you're effectively casting a spell. You need to be conscious that what you're calling in is good stuff rather than bad stuff.

You're calling in the good when you say positive and empowering statements such as:

I can.

I've got this.

Anything I want I can have.

Every day in every way more and more miracles are coming my way.

But when you disempower yourself and talk in a negative or limiting way, you're calling in more of the same. Your brain will then subconsciously find ways to prove that what you're saying is indeed true – it's that red car theory at play again!

Nothing good has come from speaking negatively, ever. It can also have a significant and detrimental effect on your emotions and behavior.

So How Do You Protect Your Mind from Negative Self-Talk?

- **Be mindful of the inner dialogue you have with yourself.** Being self-aware is everything when it comes to nipping this in the bud. The second you become aware of negative thought patterns – stop. Acknowledge them, then challenge the validity of your thoughts and ask yourself: *is there anything to support this belief?* The answer is almost always 'no.' It's rare that I speak unkindly to myself, but when I do, I quickly follow it up with an empowering statement such as: *I cancel and delete the words I just said. Instead, what I meant to say is...*

- **Pattern-interrupt by distracting yourself.** Whenever you notice yourself in a negative loop, it's a sign that you're in your head too much. The best thing you can do in instances like this is block out the sound of your own voice. Download a podcast, watch a film, listen to your favorite playlist, go for a run, meet a friend for coffee. Do anything and everything to ensure that someone else is in your ear and that person isn't you.

- **Surround yourself with positivity.** Make a list of all the things that make you feel good or bring you joy, and commit to doing as many of those things on your list as possible. Immerse yourself in good news, hang out with people who lift you up, and do a random act of kindness. When you do good things, it always comes back to you tenfold.

- **Work out.** Nothing shifts my energy quicker than getting my sweat on. When I feel stressed or down, I go for a run. Cardio workouts are great for mood boosting, as is weight training, and going for walks in nature.

Be kind to yourself always. Even on the days where you lose motivation or feel a bit *meh*. Treat yourself with the same kindness and understanding that you would offer a friend. Remember, the longest person you're ever going to be in a relationship with is you.

LIMIT YOUR CONSUMPTION OF NEGATIVE NEWS

If it doesn't inspire you, educate you, or motivate you, it's a waste of valuable time and energy.

In today's world, it can be easy to get caught up in a constant stream of negative news and actively participate in doomscrolling. Dictionary.com defines this as: 'The practice of obsessively checking online news for updates, especially on social media feeds, with the expectation that the news will be bad such that the feeling of dread from this negative expectation fuels a compulsion to continue looking for updates in a self-perpetuating cycle.'

There is no shortage of bad news that can be consumed, so unless you have a sense of heightened self-awareness and do everything you can to shield yourself from it, consuming too much will take its toll for the following reasons:

- **It can have a negative impact on your mental health, leading to increased distress, anxiety, and depression.** Studies have linked poor mental health to news exposure during negative and traumatic events, such as terrorist attacks or natural disasters; the more news a person consumes during and after these events, the more likely they are to suffer from depression, stress, and anxiety. For example, a 2014 study surveyed 4,675 Americans in the weeks following the Boston Marathon bombings and collected data on how much media they consumed. Participants who engaged with more than six hours of media coverage per day were nine times more likely to experience symptoms of high, acute stress than those who only watched a minimal amount of news.[8] An article by Robin Blades noted: 'According to Graham Davey, professor emeritus of psychology at the University of Sussex, exposure to bad news can make personal worries seem worse and even cause "acute stress reactions and some symptoms of post-traumatic stress disorder that can be quite long-lasting."'[9]

Consuming negative news can also make it difficult to focus and concentrate; and in a world where our attention spans are apparently becoming shorter, we need to do everything in our power to stay focused and minimize any distractions.

- **It can lead to a distorted view of the world.** When we're constantly bombarded with stories about crime, violence, and war, it can be easy to believe that the world is a dangerous and scary place. But the reality is that the world is a much more complex and nuanced place, with plenty of good news to be found.

A fascinating study was conducted across 105,000 different variations of news headlines that generated 5.7 million clicks on the site of the media company

Upworthy.com. Although positive words were slightly more prevalent than negative words, researchers found that: 'negative words in news headlines increased consumption rates (and positive words decreased consumption rates). For a headline of average length, each additional negative word increased the click-through rate by 2.3 percent.'[10]

- **It can lead to apathy and inaction.** When we're continuously exposed to stories about the world's problems, it can be easy to feel sad, overwhelmed, and hopeless. It could even lead us to start to think that there's nothing we can do to make a difference in the world, so why bother trying?

In another study, researchers at the University of Sussex took 30 people and split them into three groups, each of which was shown a different 14-minute news bulletin that was either positive, balanced, or negative. The participants' mood was measured before and after the film. Those who were given the negative news finished the experiment in a more anxious and sad state of mind than those who were given the positive or neutral reports. People in the negative group were also more likely to worry about their own private concerns.[11] In other words, the results suggested that watching negative news can make people worry about more than just the content of the bulletin.

Is it important to stay informed about current events and to be engaged with the struggles of others? Of course it is. But there are ways to do this and protect your mind without exposing yourself to a constant stream of negative news. One way is to limit your news consumption to a few trusted sources, who you know provide accurate and balanced reporting. You can also choose to focus on news stories that are positive or inspiring, or social media accounts that specifically focus on spreading happiness and positivity in the world.

Studies show that positive psychology interventions, such as gratitude journaling and imagining a 'best future self,' increase optimism. In one 2017 trial, patients with heart disease who received 'optimism' training reported sustained improvements in optimism, hope, life satisfaction, and anxiety between two and four months later.[12] A stronger optimistic bias also appears to confer health benefits. Optimists enjoy better physical and mental health, and are more resilient, even though they assess risk less accurately than pessimists.

Remember, the news is just one part of a much bigger story. There's a lot of good happening in the world that doesn't get reported on. My invitation to you is to make an effort to seek out positive news stories or accounts to follow, and focus on the things that are going well in your own life. Remember, part of embodying what it means to Think Like a Boss is to see yourself as the victor, not the victim. Limiting your consumption of negative news will also improve your mental health, give you a more balanced view of the world, and it'll increase your motivation to help make a difference in the world.

PROTECT YOUR MIND TIP #5

MONITOR YOUR USE OF SOCIAL MEDIA

Where you are next year is a direct result of the work you do, the content you consume, the habits you build, and the standards you set for yourself this year.

Social media isn't just a pastime – worryingly, it's now also an addiction. Recent data published by Statista confirms that 62.6 percent of the world's population is active on social media, which equates to about 5.07 billion people.[13] According to the latest research:

- The average person spends 143 minutes per day on social media.[14]

- Over 210 million users worldwide are said to be suffering from internet and social media addiction, with young adults unsurprisingly being impacted the most.[15]

- According to a recent Gallup survey of 1,500 US adolescents, 51 percent of teenagers report browsing on social media apps such as TikTok, YouTube, Instagram, Facebook, and X (formerly Twitter) for at least four hours per day.[16]

- On average, 13-year-olds were found to spend 4.1 hours per day on social media, but this figure increased to as much as 5.8 hours per day for 17-year-olds. Girls scroll for nearly one hour a day more than boys.

- Among 18- to 29-year-olds, 90 percent were found to be social media users.

- About 15 percent of 23- to 38-year-olds revealed that they are addicted to social media and this only accounts for those who were willing to admit it.

- Despite social media platforms enforcing a minimum age requirement of 13 years, more than half of children aged 11 and 12 have social media profiles.

So, What Are the Effects of Social Media Addiction?

The social media boom has led to a decline in mental health from 2011 until now, especially among young adults, according to the Youth Risk Behavior Survey conducted by the US's Center for Disease Control and Prevention. The survey found that between 1999 and 2022, suicide rates doubled for girls and increased by 50 percent for boys. Social psychologist Jonathan Haidt believes that the deterioration of mental health in young adults is a result of the rising use of smartphones and social media.[17]

Another US survey involving 6,643 parents and 1,592 adolescents was conducted by Gallup in 2023, in response to increasing concerns around the overconsumption of social media and the potential knock-on effects for mental health.[18] The survey found that teenagers who used social media apps for more than five hours a day:

- were 2.5 times more likely to harm themselves or have thoughts about suicide.

- were also 2.4 times more likely to perceive their body in a negative way.

- about 40 percent were also more likely to have felt sad the previous day.

Interestingly, these mental health findings were only associated with YouTube and TikTok, with no effects identified for Facebook, Instagram, or X (formerly Twitter). Negative self-body image, however, was strongly associated with time spent scrolling on YouTube, TikTok, Instagram, and WhatsApp.

While there are benefits of using social media, such as enhanced connection, an improved sense of belonging, and providing a powerful way to build a brand or business, it can also lead to tremendous stress, pressure to compare oneself to others, and increased sadness and isolation.

If you're a parent reading this, I beg you to monitor (and limit) your child's social media consumption. I've lost count of the number of messages I've received from teenagers who are depressed or on the brink of suicide begging for help. Worse still, their parents often have no idea! And it's either because of cyber-bullying or because they're validating their sense of self-worth from the volume of likes, comments, and followers they have.

My invitation to you as you read this chapter is to pay attention to your consumption and think about the following question:

If the average person spends 143 minutes a day on social media, can you imagine how much more you could achieve in your day if you cut your consumption down by half and poured one hour a day back into you and your goals? Imagine where you could be a year from now...

· · · · · ·

Your mind is the single most powerful weapon you own. It can be used to achieve great things and create positive change in your life. It can also be used to overcome challenges and heal from trauma. It can be a source of incredible strength, resilience, and empowerment, or it can be a source of crippling self-doubt and limitation. As we have seen in this part of the book, what you choose to focus on and how you choose to interpret events will shape your reality. If you focus on the negative, you will only see more of it. If you focus on the positive, you will find more reasons to be grateful, hopeful, and have more willingness to keep persevering. Remember, with the right mindset, there is no limit to what you can achieve.

PART V

HABITS AND ACTIONS

WIN LIKE A BOSS

Your daily actions shape your reality.

From the clothes we wear to the food we eat – every decision we make has a direct impact on our current reality. So, if you're craving a life upgrade, look at your daily habits. In this chapter, I will introduce you to habits, actions, and rituals that will not only improve your overall well-being, but they will help you Think Big, Live Big, and Win Big in life.

As you work your way through this section, I invite you to commit to a new way of being. Success is nothing without routine and routine is nothing without habit. When people aren't where they want to be, it's usually for one of two reasons: either they've not yet taken any steps to get there or they're not taking the 'right' action.

UNDERSTANDING HABITS

A habit can best be described as something you do regularly and often, usually without thinking, such as brushing your teeth, washing your face, taking a shower, or making your bed. Here are some interesting facts about habits:

- Approximately 43 percent of our daily behaviors are performed out of habit according to habit researcher Wendy Wood.[1,2]

- Habits can be broken but not forgotten. While you can replace a bad habit with a good habit, the original learned behavior will never be erased by your brain.[3] Hence why bad habits can be hard to break.

- According to James Clear, the author of *Atomic Habits*: 'On average, it takes more than two months before a new behavior becomes automatic – 66 days to be exact!'[4]

- The chances of successfully breaking a bad habit increases by over 507 percent if you continue with the new behavior for more than a year!

- On average, people make at least four attempts to break bad habits involving technology before eventually succeeding.

Why Do We Want to Instill Good Habits?

Research has proven that instilling healthy habits may, in some cases, have the following benefits:

- Increases our confidence

- Boosts our energy

- Enhances our mood

- Helps to manage stress

- Leads to healthier eating

- Improves longevity

- Enhances self-esteem

- Promotes better sleep

- Improves our focus

- Improves health

- Leads to better chances of success

Your life is essentially a compilation of your habits. So, if your behaviors sit on the positive end of the spectrum, you're winning. If they don't, then this will be contributing to where you are now, in this present moment.

The good news is that you can take control of your life by changing your habits. Bad habits can be stamped out and new habits can be formed. It just takes practice and repetition.

How Is a Habit Formed?

Before we focus on introducing good habits, it can be helpful to understand how they are formed first. Charles Duhigg, author of *The Power of Habit*, describes a pattern that is at the core of every habit.[5] This three-step loop helps us comprehend what drives our actions, and works as follows:

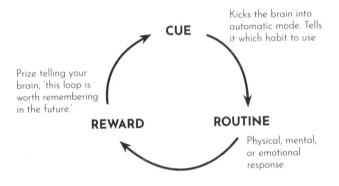

The three-step loop

1. **Cue** – is a trigger that tells your brain to go into automatic mode and which habit to use.

2. **Routine** – relates to an activity, an emotion, or a behavior and is physical, mental, or emotional.

3. **Reward** – how your brain determines if a loop is beneficial to you or not and if it's worth remembering in the future.

This loop can be manipulated to modify our behavior and habits – from midnight snacking to early morning meditating. The more often your brain loops, the more ingrained the behavior becomes. For example:

- Cue: you're feeling bored.

- Routine: you go to the kitchen and raid your snack drawer.

How to Form New Habits

The most effective way to swap out bad habits for good ones is through rewiring the brain. Specifically, by focusing on step two in the habit loop process and *replacing an old routine with a new routine*. This is known as the golden rule of habit change.

The golden rule of habit change asserts that the most powerful way to change a habit is to keep the old cue and reward, and modify only the routine. Over time and with enough repetition, the new routine becomes a new behavior. That behavior then becomes automatic and a new habit is formed.

It's typically easier to embed a new habit than it is to break an old habit, because the behavioral patterns that humans repeat become imprinted as neural pathways (signals that go from one part of the brain to another). I'm not going to dwell on why it's harder to break old habits, because I'm here to empower you to Think Like a Boss. The most important thing you need to know is that *it is possible* to build new behaviors and that's through repetition.

Habit Stacking

One of the easiest ways to build new habits by changing your routine is with a technique known as habit stacking. This term was devised by author S.J. Scott in his book of the same name. Habit stacking occurs when you add a new behavior to an existing one. This then makes the new behavior easier to stick to because you're not introducing an entirely new routine or activity. You're merely building a new habit on top of an old one.

Example goal: start flossing teeth to improve oral hygiene.

- Existing habit: brushing teeth

- New habit: flossing teeth

You can habit stack by introducing the new behavior of flossing into your existing routine of cleaning your teeth. Provided you keep repeating this behavior every time you brush your teeth, flossing will become a new habit before long.

Tips for habit stacking

- **Start small.** Don't try to add too many new habits at once. Choose one or two habits to focus on and add them to your routine gradually.

- **Choose habits that are compatible.** The habits you stack should be compatible with each other. For example, if you're trying to eat healthier you could habit stack by eating a healthy snack after you work out.

- **Be consistent.** The key to habit stacking is to be consistent. Try to perform the new habit at the same time each day.

Habit stacking is a powerful technique that can really change your game when it comes to improving your life and achieving your goals.

If it doesn't serve you,

it's time to let it go.

SETTING YOURSELF
UP FOR SUCCESS

My first tip for setting yourself up to win is to delete, throw away, or remove anything that could hinder your progress when it comes to building new habits. It's easier to revert back to an old habit than it is to form a new habit because your brain never forgets a learned behavior – especially one that you've done on autopilot for a long time. You therefore want to do everything within your power to give yourself the best possible chance for success.

Let's take healthy eating as an example. If you've set the intention to eat a more nutritious diet, consider throwing away any food or drinks that could either tempt you, hinder your progress, or set you back, such as fizzy drinks, cakes, chocolates, sweets, and ultra-processed foods.

When people revert back to bad habits it's usually down to one or more of the following reasons:

- they lack commitment
- they don't have a strong enough purpose
- they don't have accountability
- they start too big and too abruptly

- they have no means of tracking their progress as a means of incentivizing themselves.

Start Your Day the Right Way: Focus Like a Boss

How you start your morning sets the tone for the rest of your day. One of the most important rules I live my life by is not to look at my mobile phone in the first one to two hours of waking up because it can impact my productivity (we all know how easy it can be to get lost in the scroll!) and it just doesn't make me feel good.

Science has also confirmed that using your phone too soon after waking up, can impact your mental health. You see, waking up uses multiple different brain waves, all of which play a key role in your overall well-being. Jay Rai, an empowerment psychologist, states that when you first wake up, for example, your brain switches from delta waves (which are resting and regenerative) to theta waves (which are key for learning and development, making memories, and processing information).[6] If you check your phone too soon, you're forcing your brain to bypass from a delta state to beta brain waves – which forces your brain to skip out on those all-important alpha and theta brain waves. This can then result in an onset of negative side effects throughout the rest of your day. For more on brain waves, please see *Self-Love Tip #5: Protect Your Energy: Not Everyone Deserves Access to You*, p.123.

If you check your phone first thing and are bombarded with an influx of notifications, you're more likely to start your day feeling behind and overwhelmed. You're also more likely to see negative news sooner, especially if your notifications are turned on.

One thing I highly recommend is enabling the Focus function on your phone. As with Do Not Disturb mode, where all incoming messages and calls are silenced – except from people on your priority list, like children or parents – you can also set it to switch off notifications from apps. Each evening at 9 p.m. my phone defaults to Focus. The only exception is if I manually click into my phone settings and disable the function, which rarely happens. My Focus mode then lasts for 12 hours, because that's how I set it up. At 9 a.m., my Focus mode automatically disables and I start receiving inbound calls and messages.

Now, to avoid overstimulating my brain once 9 a.m. hits, the majority of my notifications remain turned off. I only receive notifications from a very small number of apps – all of which I consider to be important and all of which are related to health or work. I receive zero notifications from news apps, zero notifications from messaging apps (like WhatsApp), and zero notifications from social media apps, including Instagram. This is intentional. I'm *very disciplined* about what I am and am not available for, especially during working hours. I'm also proactive, as opposed to reactive, and I encourage you to be the same.

As someone with a large social media following, it's normal for my social media content to receive thousands of interactions every day – from likes and comments, to story shout-outs and DMs. Sometimes the volume can go into the tens of thousands, especially if a piece of content goes viral!

Can you imagine how crazy my brain would be if my phone was vibrating every second of the day, just from social media notifications?! Just thinking about it is overwhelming. Which is why I made the empowering decision a few years ago to turn off all my social media notifications. It's one of the best things I've ever done for my mental well-being and not once have I been tempted to reverse it. Getting distracted by likes, comments, and messages, is not an efficient use of your time nor does it pay the bills. It can also be detrimental to your focus and productivity.

In fact, in an interview published by Gallup, Gloria Mark, an associate professor at the University of California, Irvine, confirmed that a study found it took on average 23 minutes and 15 seconds to get back to work after an interruption.[7] This means that even if you're only distracted a few times a day, you still lose at least an hour of work! Even the prospect of an interruption can have a detrimental effect on your ability to focus. An article published in the *Journal of the Association for Consumer Research* found that if your smartphone is close at hand while you're working, your performance and cognitive capacity can be affected even if you don't receive any messages or notifications![8] No wonder we so often feel behind as a society or like we don't have enough time, so we end up working on the weekends to compensate and catch up.

In case you need any more convincing as to how your mobile phone could be blocking your progress, here are some alarming facts that a recent survey by the consumer website Reviews.org uncovered about mobile phone usage among Americans:[9]

- Within 10 minutes after waking in the morning, 89 percent admitted to checking their mobile phone.

- They check their phones on average 144 times per day and spend an average of 4 hours and 25 minutes on their phones. This is up by 30 percent from 2022, when they used their phones daily for 2 hours and 54 minutes.

- After receiving a notification, 75 percent checked their phones within five minutes and 75 percent also used their phone while on the toilet.

- If the phone battery slipped beneath 20 percent, 47 percent of Americans felt anxious or panicked.

- One in six respondents sleep with their phone nearby during the night.

- Nearly 57 percent of those questioned considered themselves to be mobile phone addicts. Indeed, '55 percent say that they have never gone longer than 24 hours without their cell phone.'

- The survey also found that '46 percent use or look at their phone while on a date.'

- Alarmingly, '27 percent use or look at their phone while driving.'

The motto of the story: Think Like a Boss and limit your mobile phone usage, especially if you want to make more room in your day to focus on activities that will help you Think Big, Live Big, and Win Big!

Drive gets you going, but discipline keeps you growing.

QUALITIES YOU NEED TO WIN BIG

Here are five things that people who achieve more do:

1. They are disciplined enough to do things without needing to be told

They drive themselves to get things done, even when they're tired or have no motivation, because they are committed to reaching the end goal. Self-disciplined people also typically approach their tasks in an organized, deliberate, and thorough manner. People with a strong sense of self-discipline are also able to:

- stick to their goals or commitments even when it's difficult

- stay focused on their tasks, despite distractions

- delay immediate gratification by passing on short-term wins for long-term gains

- control their emotions and reactions

2. They are driven because they want to succeed

They motivate themselves to keep striving for their goals. Driven people also have an innate desire to be the best they can possibly be. Their desire to succeed drives their motivation and they are typically also:

- clear on what they want
- determined to accomplish what they set their mind to
- passionate about their goals
- confident in their abilities
- not afraid to step out of their comfort zone

3. They are persistent and keep going

Come rain or snow, they show up for themselves. Think about the character that Sylvester Stallone plays in the *Rocky* franchise. Rocky Balboa is relentless – even when he's blue in the face and appears to be losing the biggest boxing match of his career. He perseveres until the end and eventually wins. Persistent people have the ability to keep going, even when things are tough and they're faced with challenges and setbacks. People who are persistent are also:

- willing to put the hard work in to achieve their goals
- not afraid of failure
- able to learn from their mistakes
- determined to succeed

4. They are patient

They also have the ability to stay calm and focused, even when they're not yet seeing results or when things are taking longer than expected. People who are patient are also:

- trusting of the process
- aware that some things take time
- good at active listening
- better at coping with stress
- don't appear to get easily frustrated

5. They are resilient and mentally strong

They are able to bounce back from setbacks and disappointments. They don't let adversity define them and they keep going. They know that their purpose is bigger than their goal, so they find strength by moving beyond themselves. They also see negative experiences as only temporary. People who display resilience are also typically:

- able to problem-solve
- have a survivor's mentality
- see themselves as a victor not a victim
- able to regulate their emotions
- don't let adversity define them

Winning Habits

You don't need to make life-changing moves to see life-changing results. What you do need, however, is to take action and be consistent. Then little by little, a little becomes a lot. In the next section, I share the habits that will help you to win BIG...

Winners don't quit and
quitters don't win.

PRACTICE GRATITUDE

Start each day with a grateful heart.

Like many of us growing up, I was educated to say 'please' and 'thank you' for everything. It's a habit that we have ingrained in our psyche and say on autopilot whenever we receive something. It wasn't until several years ago, when I read *The Secret* by Rhonda Byrne, however, that I really started to grasp the concept of finding gratitude in everything: both the good and the bad.

If you're unfamiliar with this concept or practice, then gratitude is simply appreciating what you have, instead of reflecting on what you don't have. There are a lot of complainers in the world and all complaining does is lower the vibration of the planet and attract more people who complain. I'm unavailable for low-vibe Negative Nellies – and so should you be. If everyone in the world actually stopped for a minute and reflected on the positives, acknowledging everything that's going well for them, then they would attract more positivity and good things into their life, and the benefits don't stop there. So, how can the world benefit from practicing daily gratitude?

- **Gratitude can enhance mental well-being.** Research shows that practicing gratitude for 15 minutes a day, five days a week, for at least six weeks, can enhance mental wellness and possibly promote a lasting change in perspective.[10] Gratitude can also positively affect your physical health.

- **Gratitude reduces depression.** A review of 70 studies that include responses from more than 26,000 people found a significant association between higher levels of gratitude and lower levels of depression.[11] Gratitude seems to reduce depression symptoms, as people with a grateful mindset report a higher satisfaction with life, strong social relationships, and greater self-esteem than those who don't practice gratitude.

- **Gratitude lessens anxiety.** Anxiety often involves worrying and negative thinking. Gratitude can be a coping tool for anxiety. Regularly practicing gratitude combats negative thinking patterns by keeping thoughts focused on the present. If you find yourself focusing on negative thoughts about the past or future, challenge yourself to find something you are grateful for now. It will break the negative thought process and return you to the present moment.

- **Gratitude supports heart health.** Several studies show that a grateful mindset positively affects biomarkers associated with the risk of heart disease. In 2016, a sample of patients with heart disease took part in a study where they did eight weeks of gratitude journaling. The results highlighted that their biomarker concentrations reduced significantly in the gratitude intervention group, compared to the treatment-as-usual group.[12] Having grateful thoughts, even if you don't write them down, is said to help your heart by slowing and regulating your breathing to synchronize with your heartbeat.

- **Relieves stress.** When we feel stressed, it triggers a fight-or-flight response in the body, resulting in a faster heartbeat and more adrenaline running through the nervous system. Practicing gratitude can help to calm the nervous system as it causes physiological changes to the area of the body that helps you rest and digest. Gratitude and the response it causes can help to reduce your heart rate and blood pressure, and supports overall relaxation.

Tips for Practicing Gratitude

- **Keep a gratitude journal.** Write down three things you are grateful for each day at a minimum (*see Win Like a Boss Tip #8, p.209*).

- **Practice mindfulness.** Pay attention to the present moment and appreciate the simple things in life or the things we often take for granted, like a delicious meal or a warm shower (*see Win Like a Boss Tip #4, p.199*).

- **Be of service to others.** Helping others is a great way to cultivate an attitude of gratitude.

- **Express your gratitude to others.** Let the people in your life know how much you appreciate them.

Physical benefits of gratitude

- **An improved immune system.** Studies have shown that grateful people are less likely to get sick. This is because gratitude has been shown to boost the immune system.[13]

- **Better sleep.** Grateful people are more likely to get a good night's sleep. This is because gratitude helps to reduce stress and anxiety, which can both interfere with sleep.

- **Reduces pain.** Grateful people are less likely to experience pain. This is because gratitude has been shown to reduce inflammation, which is a major cause of pain.[14]

- **Lower blood pressure.** Grateful people are less likely to have high blood pressure. This is because gratitude has been shown to lower stress levels, which can lead to lower blood pressure.

Mental benefits of gratitude

- **Increased happiness.** Grateful people are more likely to be happy. This is because gratitude has been shown to increase positive emotions and decrease negative emotions.

- **Reduced stress.** Grateful people are less likely to experience stress. This is because gratitude helps to put things in perspective and makes us less likely to dwell on negative events.

- **Improved self-esteem.** Grateful people are more likely to have high self-esteem because gratitude helps us focus on our strengths and accomplishments.

- **Increased resilience.** Grateful people are more likely to be resilient in the face of challenge. This is because gratitude helps us to develop a positive outlook on life and see challenges as opportunities for growth.

Emotional benefits of gratitude

- **Stronger relationships.** Grateful people are more likely to have strong relationships because gratitude helps us to appreciate the people in our lives and express our love for them.

- **More compassion.** Grateful people are more likely to be compassionate toward others because gratitude helps us to understand the suffering of others and makes us want to help them.

- **Greater sense of purpose.** Grateful people are more likely to have a greater sense of purpose in life, because gratitude helps us to connect with our values and see how our lives are making a difference in the world.

PRIORITIZE YOUR SLEEP

*'Sleep is the single most effective thing we can
do to reset our brain and body health every day.'*
MATTHEW WALKER

If only my younger self knew what I know now, I probably wouldn't have spent the best part of my 20s sleep deprived. I wish I could tell you it's because I was out having fun. But the reality is I wasn't. I, like so many others, succumbed to the pressure of my career. The long hours and unrealistic demands of my role meant I was always overstretched, and the only choice I felt that I had was to work longer hours, in the hope it would reduce the volume of work. I wince now, when I reflect on the long-term effects of sleep deprivation. So, if you're not currently averaging the recommended seven to nine hours sleep per night because of your career, your lifestyle, or because you're a parent to young children (where sleep is temporarily out of your control), you might be interested to know the following:

- **Sleep deprivation can be deadly.** People can survive much longer without food than they can without sleep. So, if you ever need to choose between eating and getting some rest, you might want to go with the latter![15]

- **Sleep strengthens your immune system.** If you don't get enough sleep, you increase your chances of catching a virus the following day. So if you want to stay healthy, make sure you get at least seven hours of rest!

- **You can't catch up on sleep.** A Harvard study showed that sleeping extra hours after an extended period without any sleep decreased reaction times and the ability to focus.[16] So make sure you regularly sleep for at least seven hours every day.

- **There are over 100 recognized sleep disorders.** They come in four different categories: difficulty falling/staying asleep, difficulty staying awake, difficulty maintaining a sleep schedule, and unusual behaviors during sleep. From common insomnia to rare narcolepsy, a lot can go wrong when it comes to sleeping.

- **All-nighters can decrease your performance.** While staying up all night to study for an exam might be tempting, it can have a big impact on your well-being and subsequent performance.

What Happens When You Don't Get Enough Sleep

Poor sleep impacts cognitive function in a variety of ways.

Short-term results of lack of sleep:

- difficulty concentrating
- decline in mood
- impaired memory

- visible signs of fatigue

Long-term results of poor sleep:

- poor work performance

- cognitive decline

- heightened risk of dementia

In addition to the impact of lack of sleep outlined above, there are other findings:

- **You're adding inches to your waistline.** Believe it or not, by getting the recommended amount of sleep each night you could lose some weight! A 2017 study found that people who sleep on average six hours a night had a waist measurement that was on average more than an inch (3cm) greater than that of people who were sleeping for nine hours or more a night. Now here's where things get interesting... there appeared to be no correlation between less sleep and a less healthy diet, which surprised researchers, since most previous studies suggested that less sleep can lead to poor diet choices. The findings of the study suggests that a lack of sleep could be an exclusive culprit of weight gain![17]

- **You lower good cholesterol levels.** According to the same study, people who sleep less than the recommended number of hours and average just six hours or less a night also had reduced levels of HDL cholesterol – this is our good cholesterol. HDL cholesterol helps to eliminate fat from circulation, which is important in protecting us from heart disease.

- **You cave in to more cravings.** Several studies have shown that not getting enough sleep leads to more calories being consumed. Findings from a 2016 study undertaken by researchers at King's College, London highlighted that people who don't sleep enough consume an average of 385 more calories per day than those who get the recommended amount of sleep.[18]

- **You increase your risk of obesity and heart disease.** Interruptions to your sleep and your internal body clock (also known as your circadian rhythm) can increase your risk of diseases and disorders, including obesity, dementia, and heart disease, according to the US's National Institute of Health.[19]

- **Your reaction times suffer.** Unsurprisingly, poor sleep can impactive our cognitive functioning, impacting productivity and leading to slower reaction times, according to the US's National Heart, Lung and Blood Institute.[20] When you don't get enough rest, your ability to make decisions suffers because your brain hasn't had enough time to repair, leaving you feeling tired and weary. It can also lead to a sharp decline in learning and memory tasks.

- **You're more likely to think negative thoughts.** A study from Binghamton University, New York, found that sleeping less than the recommended average of eight hours a night is linked with invasive thoughts, similar to those who suffer from anxiety and depression.[21] Sleep deprivation can result in people struggling to shift their attention away from negative information, researchers found. Their findings suggest that inadequate sleep contributes to making negative thoughts stick around.

How to Practice Good Sleep Hygiene

Sleep hygiene refers to the habits and practices that can help you get a good night's sleep. Good sleep hygiene will help you to fall asleep more easily, stay asleep longer, and wake up feeling refreshed. Here are some tips to support you in getting a better night's sleep:

- **Establish a regular sleep schedule.** Go to bed and wake up at the same time every day, even on weekends. This can help regulate your body's internal clock.

- **Create a relaxing bedtime routine.** Engage in calming activities before bed such as reading, having a bubble bath, or listening to relaxing music.

- **Optimize your sleep environment.** Ensure your bedroom is dark, quiet, and cool. Use blackout curtains, earplugs, and a white-noise machine if necessary.

- **Avoid stimulants in the evening.** Limit caffeine and alcohol consumption in the hours leading up to your bedtime, as these substances can interfere with sleep.

- **Get regular exercise.** Exercise is beneficial for sleep but avoid vigorous workouts too close to bedtime.

- **Limit your screen time before bed.** The blue light emitted from electronic devices can disrupt sleep. Avoid looking at a bright screen two to three hours before bed and turn off your screens at least one hour (but ideally two hours) before bedtime. For more on a bedtime routine see *Win Like a Boss Tip #10, Evening Routine* on p.222.

- **Create a comfortable sleep environment.** Invest in a comfortable mattress, pillows, and bedding.

- **See a doctor if sleep problems persist.** If you're experiencing chronic sleep problems, consult a healthcare professional.

As you can see, prioritizing sleep is essential for optimal brain function and overall health. By making sleep a priority, you're investing in your physical, mental, and emotional well-being. Think Like a Boss and get more sleep!

MEDITATE

'Listen to silence, it has so much to say.'

RUMI

Meditation is a practice that originates from India's ancient Vedic era and has been used for centuries to promote calmness, relaxation, and contemplation; reduce stress; and improve overall well-being. This practice involves training the mind to focus on the present moment, without judgment or attachment.

There are many different ways to meditate and they all involve some form of focused attention. This could be focusing on your breath, a mantra, or a physical sensation.

Tips for Starting to Meditate

- **Find a quiet place.** Choose a comfortable and quiet space where you won't be disturbed.

- **Set a timer.** Start with a short duration, such as three minutes, and gradually increase the time as you become more accustomed with this practice.

- **Sit in a comfortable position.** Either cross-legged on the floor or on a cushion, or in a chair with your feet flat on the floor.

- **Close your eyes.** This will help you to block out distractions and focus on your inner experience.

- **Focus on your breath.** Begin by paying attention to your breath. Notice the sensation of air entering and leaving your body.

- **Let go of expectations.** Don't expect to have a specific experience or reach a certain state of mind. Simply observe your thoughts and sensations without judgment.

- **Download an app.** There are some great apps that offer guided meditations to get you started. Two of my go-to's are Calm and Headspace. If you're looking for something a bit different, I highly recommend trying Superhuman Activations. This is a visualization-focused audio app that energizes and inspires the listener. Different to meditations, Activations are designed to be listened to in everyday moments.

- **Be patient.** Meditation takes practice. Don't be discouraged if you find it difficult at first. Just keep practicing and you will eventually see its benefits.

When you practice meditation regularly, you can cultivate a greater sense of calm, clarity, and inner peace.

Benefits of Practicing Meditation

- **Reduced stress and anxiety.** Meditation has been shown to reduce levels of cortisol, a stress hormone, and increase levels of serotonin, a mood-boosting neurotransmitter. In a study, researchers from John Hopkins University identified that general meditation programs helped to alleviate symptoms of depression, anxiety, and pain.[22] In a separate study at Google and Roche, employees were required to use a meditation app such as Headspace (which offers meditation routines) for eight weeks and participants reported a 46 percent reduction in depression and a 31 percent reduction in anxiety.[23]

- **Improved focus and concentration.** Meditation can help us to train our attention and improve our ability to focus on the present moment. One study found that people who used a meditation app for four weeks improved their focus by 14 percent, while another study reported that one single session could reduce mind-wandering by 22 percent.[24, 25]

- **Increased self-awareness.** Meditation can help us become more aware of our thoughts, feelings, and sensations. When we meditate, we practice focusing on our breath, body sensations, or a mantra, which helps to calm the mind and reduce distractions. This allows us to observe our thoughts, feelings, and sensations without judgment, which can lead to greater self-awareness and understanding.

- **Improved emotional regulation.** Meditation can teach us how to manage our emotions in a healthy way. This can lead to more positive and fulfilling relationships with others. Interestingly, in another study, 153 adults who used a mindfulness meditation app for two weeks, reported reduced feelings of loneliness and increased social contact compared with those in a control group.[26]

- **Enhanced creativity and problem-solving.** Meditation can help us access our intuition and open up our minds to new possibilities. This can lead to more creative and innovative thinking.

- **Greater sense of well-being.** Meditation can help us connect with our inner peace and happiness, which can lead to a more fulfilling and meaningful life. Studies have also demonstrated the link between practicing short guided meditations several times a week and participants reporting better outcomes related to work-related stress and well-being.[27]

There are many benefits of meditation and there are plenty of resources, such as apps, articles, classes, and books available to help you get started. With regular practice, you can experience these benefits for yourself.

MINDFULNESS

'Quiet the mind and the soul will speak.'

MA JAYA SATI BHAGAVATI

Mindfulness is the practice of paying attention to the present moment and being aware of your thoughts, your feelings, and your surroundings, without being reactive or getting distracted by what's going on around you. People have been engaging in mindfulness for centuries. The term originates from the Buddhist concept of Sati (not to be confused with the Hindu term), which relates to the 'moment to moment awareness of present events,' according to Wikipedia.[28] The modern term 'mindfulness' emerged in 1881 when Thomas William Rhys Davids, a British magistrate in Sri Lanka (previously known as Ceylon), identified 'mindfulness' as the closest English translation of the Buddhist concept of Sati. While mindfulness has been widely practiced in the East for hundreds of years, it didn't make its way over to the West until the 1970s.

Mindfulness is a powerful tool that can help us reduce stress, improve our focus, and increase our overall well-being. Investing time on a daily basis to connect with your mind and body is one of the kindest things you can do for your physical, emotional, and spiritual well-being, as not only can this reduce stress and anxiety, but research has found that mindfulness also promotes better sleep and helps to regulate your nervous system.[29]

How Does Mindfulness Work?

Mindfulness works by training our attention to stay focused on the present moment. When we practice mindfulness, we learn to observe our thoughts and feelings without getting caught up in them. This allows us to gain a greater sense of clarity and control over our minds.

Benefits of mindfulness

- reduced stress and anxiety

- improved focus and concentration

- increased self-awareness

- improved decision-making

- increased creativity

- greater sense of well-being

Tips for practicing mindfulness

- **Meditation.** In mindfulness, you often practice meditation by sitting quietly and focusing on your breath, body sensations, or on a mantra (see *Win Like a Boss Tip #3, p.195*).

- **Yoga.** You move your body in a mindful way during yoga exercises.

- **Tai chi.** This is a slow-moving martial art that emphasizes mindfulness.

- **Walking meditation.** This is where you walk slowly and pay attention to your surroundings.

- **Mindful eating.** This is where you eat slowly and savor every bite of whatever you eat.

How Often Should You Practice Mindfulness?

Even a few minutes each day can make a big difference. As with anything, the more you practice, the greater the benefits you'll experience. Aim to practice mindfulness for at least 10 minutes every day.

How to Incorporate Mindfulness into Your Everyday Life

There are many different ways you can do this. Here are a few ideas:

- take a few minutes to meditate each morning

- practice mindful breathing throughout the day

- take a mindful walk in nature

- eat your meals mindfully

- pause and take a few deep breaths before reacting to a stressful situation

Mindfulness is a simple but powerful practice that can have a profound effect on your life. By practicing mindfulness, you can learn to live in the present moment, reduce stress and anxiety, and improve your overall well-being.

TAKE CARE OF YOUR BODY

Remember, no one's ever said, 'I really regret eating healthier today!'

Eating well and nurturing your body through proper care can help you live a longer, healthier, and more fulfilling life. It's also one of the most powerful ways you can love your body and express gratitude for what it does for you. When you eat healthy foods you're acknowledging that you care about your well-being, which can lead to the following benefits:

- **Improved mood.** Eating a healthy diet and exercising regularly can help to improve your mood and reduce symptoms of depression and anxiety. A 2017 study that assessed participants who were diagnosed with moderate to severe depression, found that their symptoms improved when they received nutritional counseling and ate a healthier diet over a 12-week period.[30] The improved diet focused on fresh whole foods and restricted processed foods, including junk food. In 32 percent of cases, mood and anxiety improved enough to achieve remission criteria in the participants. The findings highlight that symptoms of depression can be managed or improved by making changes to your diet and by exercising regularly.

- **Increased energy levels.** Eating a healthy diet and getting enough sleep can give you more energy throughout your day.

- **Reduced risk of diseases.** Eating a healthy diet and exercising regularly can help to reduce your risk of developing chronic, and other, diseases such as heart disease, strokes, type 2 diabetes, and some types of cancer. The charity Cancer Research UK states that while not all cancers can be prevented, we can take actions to reduce our risk, and this includes keeping to a healthy weight, being active, avoiding sunburn, and not smoking.[31]

MOVE YOUR BODY

Calm your mind.

One thing I do every day without fail is move my body. Whether it's walking, running, hiking, weight training, yoga, or attending a gym class. Not only does movement contribute to our overall well-being, but there are countless scientific studies on the additional benefits. Particularly when it comes to mental health and mood disorders such as depression. A recent study has found exercise to be an effective remedy for treating people with depression. What's more, walking, jogging, yoga, and strength training could be considered core treatments for improving symptoms of depression along with psychotherapy and antidepressants.[32]

Experts analyzed 14,170 people with a major depression disorder from 218 separate trials and ranked different forms of exercise by how effective they were at treating the condition compared with existing treatments. While all forms of intervention were effective to some degree, the study found that taking antidepressants known as selective serotonin reuptake inhibitors (SSRIs) – the most commonly prescribed medicine – on their own was less effective than either exercise or therapy. Researchers also found that the benefits from exercise tended to be proportional to the intensity and that the more vigorous the exercise, the better.

A record 8.6 million people in England were prescribed antidepressants from 2022 to 2023,[33] while as many as one in six people have symptoms of moderate or severe depression, according to the Office for National Statistics (ONS).[34] Exercise is also being prescribed by doctors, with the National Institute for Health and Care Excellence (NICE) recommending group exercise sessions at least once a week for 10 weeks with a trained practitioner.[35]

Tips on How to Move Your Body When You Don't Want To

- **Set realistic goals.** Don't try to do too much too soon. Start small with achievable goals, such as walking or jogging for 10 minutes every day.

- **Make it fun.** Find an activity that you enjoy and that you're likely to stick with. If you don't like running, don't force yourself to do it. There are plenty of other ways to get exercise, such as swimming, cycling, or dancing.

- **Find a workout buddy.** Having someone to work out with can help you stay motivated. Find a friend, family member, or coworker who is also interested in getting fit.

- **Make it a habit.** The more you exercise, the easier it will become. Try to make exercise a regular part of your routine, such as working out first thing in the morning or after work.

- **Reward yourself.** When you reach a goal, reward yourself with something you enjoy, such as a massage, a new outfit, or a night out with friends.

- **Don't give up.** There will be days when you don't feel like working out. That's okay. If we constantly relied on our mood to get things done, we wouldn't get much done! The key is to persevere and not give up. Even a little bit of exercise is better than no exercise at all.

- **Listen to your body.** If you're feeling pain, stop exercising and rest. You know your body better than anyone, so listen to it and avoid overdoing things.

- **Be patient.** It takes time to see results because it's a compound effect. Don't get discouraged if you don't see changes immediately. Just keep at it and before long you will start to look and feel different.

The motto of the story: if you're serious about leading a happier life, improving your mental well-being, and showing up as your best possible self – move your body.

VISUALIZATION

'If my mind can conceive it and my heart can believe it, then I can achieve it.'

MUHAMMAD ALI

Visualization is a powerful technique that involves forming a clear mental image of a desire or goal. It's a form of mental rehearsal that can help you improve your performance and accomplish your goals. Think of it a little like daydreaming. By visualizing the outcome that you want, you can start to prep your mind to succeed.

How Does It Work?

Visualization works by stimulating the same neural pathways and parts of the brain that you use when performing a physical task. When you visualize yourself carrying out a task, your brain creates a roadmap that then helps you perform the task more effectively. Visualization is also said to help improve your focus and concentration, as well as reduce stress and anxiety.

Children are amazing at visualizing and manifesting their deepest desires because they haven't yet been conditioned by societal norms. Their innocence and imagination enables them to visualize and dream about what they want because in their mind, they believe that anything is possible.

How to use visualization

Visualization is favored by many of the world's GOATs (greatest of all time). Here are five simple steps to follow if you're new to this practice:

1. **Find a quiet place** – somewhere you can relax and focus without being disturbed.

2. **Close your eyes and focus on your breathing for a few minutes.** This will help to relax your body.

3. **Set your intention.** Get clear on what you want to manifest and using your imagination, visualize yourself performing the task or achieving the goal that you desire.

4. **Engage your senses.** Play out the scene as vividly as possible and create a mental image inside your head of your desired outcome. What do you see, hear, smell, taste, and feel? Feel the emotions that you would feel if you had already reached your goal.

5. **Repeat this process as often as possible** (ideally daily) and once you've achieved your desired outcome, visualize your next goal.

By using visualization regularly, you can create a more positive and successful life.

JOURNALING

'Journaling is like whispering to yourself and listening at the same time.'

MINA MURRAY

One of my favorite tools for looking after my mental health and for giving my thoughts a voice is journaling. The term journaling is just another way of saying writing. To journal your thoughts or to write about your thoughts are one and the same. When we journal, we record our thoughts, feelings, and experiences in a private space (our journal). This simple yet profound practice can have a life-changing impact on your health – particularly on your mental and emotional well-being. I swear by this practice and it's been a staple in my daily routine for several years now. I like to journal twice a day – once in the morning and once in the evening.

There are a few different ways that you can log journal entries: the traditional way is by putting pen to paper, or you can digitally record your thoughts on an app. If you're more of a digital lover, head to the local app store on your mobile phone and search using the term 'journaling.' You'll see a number of different app options to select from and download. I personally love the traditional method, but be open to trying both and see which suits you best.

Different Types of Journaling

There are different types of journaling practices, such as reflective and gratitude journaling:

Reflective journaling

This is where you write about your life experiences and your perception of those experiences. Take each experience and ask:

- What happened?
- How did the experience play out?
- How did I react?
- Was the experience positive or negative?
- What did I learn and what can I take forward from it?
- Is there anything I would do differently next time?

Here's an example:

Today is my last day at work. I have conflicting feelings about how I feel. On the one hand I'm excited because I've felt unhappy in my role for a long time. I'm also grateful to finally be free to work for myself. But on the other hand, I'm petrified. What if it doesn't work out? What would I do? I want to make it work, really I do, but I definitely have worries. Do I even know what I'm doing?!

Part of me knows that I'm good at what I do, but running my own business is a whole other ball game. I'm just going to ensure that I learn as much as I can about how to run a successful business and learn from people who've walked my path before.

Gratitude journaling

This is the practice of writing, recording, and reflecting on things that you're grateful for. Writing in a gratitude journal or journaling about gratitude is a beautiful way of consciously acknowledging the good in life. This form of journaling is popular in the field of positive psychology and is a key part of my morning and evening routines, which you'll read about later in this chapter. For more on gratitude, see *Win Like a Boss Tip #1, Practice Gratitude*, p.184.

When I reflect on my day in my journal, I combine both types of journaling, keep it short and simple, and write about:

- three things that went well that day
- three areas that I could improve on
- three things that I'm grateful for

Notice how I keep my language empowering. I could have suggested *journal on three things that went badly or three things that didn't go so well*; instead I choose to see everything as a teaching or a learning. Empower yourself always and choose to see the positives in everything.

Here are some examples of what I may write in my journal:

Three things that went well today:

- I ran 3 miles (5km).

- I onboarded a new client.

- I received a beautiful message of gratitude from someone in my community.

Three areas where I can improve:

- drink more water, especially after running

- cut down on my sugar intake

- be more proactive rather than reactive; leave my phone in a different room when I'm working tomorrow.

Three things that I'm grateful for:

- I'm so happy and grateful that I was gifted a free coffee today.

- I'm so happy and grateful that the sun came out today.

- I'm so happy and grateful for my friends who check in on me daily.

Benefits of Journaling

- **Eases stress.** Journaling can be a powerful self-development tool for reducing stress and regulating your nervous system. Giving yourself a safe space to voice your thoughts, challenges, or stresses can be a cathartic release; it can help you process and release any pent-up emotions. Journaling also provides you with a safe space to explore your feelings without the risk of judgment, thereby promoting emotional healing and growth.

- **Reduces anxiety and depression.** Studies have shown that journaling can be an effective coping mechanism for individuals struggling with anxiety and depression.[36] Specifically, research suggests that expressive writing and gratitude journaling can reduce symptoms of depression, providing an effective intervention for clients receiving treatment in therapy. Writing about our worries and fears can help us gain perspective, develop strategies for managing difficult emotions, and cultivate a more positive outlook on life.

- **Promotes gratitude and mindfulness.** Not only can journaling cultivate a gratitude mindset, but it also promotes mindfulness by encouraging us to focus on the positive aspects of our lives. Writing about things we are grateful for and practicing mindfulness through journaling can lead to increased happiness and contentment.

- **Increases self-awareness.** One of the primary benefits of journaling is the enhanced self-awareness it brings. Writing about our experiences enables us to gain a deeper understanding of our thoughts, emotions, and motivations. It can also help us identify patterns in our behavior and recognize our strengths and weaknesses.

- **Inspires creativity and problem-solving.** By writing freely and without limits, we can feel inspired by new ideas and become more focused on solving problems and developing solutions. Journaling can also serve as a catalyst for inspiring our creativity through writing, such as writing poetry, and other forms of art.

- **Improved communication skills.** Journaling allows us to express ourselves more clearly, openly, and honestly. It also helps us to develop our listening skills and become more empathetic. Writing regularly can also enhance our vocabulary, grammar, and overall writing proficiency.

- **Better physical health.** Journaling has been linked to a number of physical health benefits, including reduced stress levels, improved quality of sleep, and a stronger immune system – thereby positively impacting our overall health and well-being.

Despite the host of benefits that journaling provides, it can feel uncomfortable at times. Especially in vulnerable moments where you're reflecting on or uncovering emotions that you may have been suppressing or avoiding. Below are some guidelines to support you in getting started.

Tips to Start Journaling

- **Start small.** Set yourself a goal of journaling three or four times a week – with 10 minutes of writing time and five minutes of reflection time as an example. You can then increase your journaling sessions and length over time.

- **There is no wrong way to journal.** The key is to get started: give yourself permission to write and explore the inner workings of your mind and see what surfaces for you.

- **Journal at a time where you won't be disturbed.** Decide on a time of day that suits you best. This could be first thing in the morning or just before bedtime. You're more likely to stick to a habit when you make it work for you.

- **Choose what you want to write about.** If you need some inspiration, use the journaling prompts below to help you.

- **Allow yourself to be vulnerable and go deep.** Remember that this is your safe space and the only person who'll read what you write is you.

- **Be kind to yourself.** If you're writing about a bad day or an unpleasant experience, this may trigger certain emotions for you. Allow yourself to feel what you feel, and don't forget to seek the support of an expert if needed.

Here are some of my favorites to get you started...

FAVORITE JOURNALING PROMPTS

- I'm at my happiest when...
- Things that make me smile are...
- I'm at my best when...
- The words I need to hear right now are...
- What three qualities do I admire about myself most?

- If I could tell my younger self anything, what would it be?
- Today I'm proud of myself for...
- What does my 'perfect day' look like? Write about it.
- How can I nourish my mind more?
- How can I nourish my body more?
- What does success mean to me?
- What can I do today to step into the person I'm becoming?
- What am I most afraid of?
- What am I most excited by?
- I forgive myself for...
- I no longer need...
- What five things would I do in life right now if I wasn't scared?
- Write 20 positive statements about yourself.
- Make a list of 10 reasons why you are worthy of more.
- Make a list of 10 things you can do to help you unwind from the craziness of life.
- What would you do if you knew you couldn't fail?
- How can I empower myself more?
- How can I be kinder to myself?
- Who would I be if I already had everything I desired and how can I embody that person today?
- Why am I not where I want to be yet? What is stopping me? Explore any blocks, limitations, or worries around your desire.
- Journal on the best-case scenario for the thing that you're most worried about at the moment that may be stopping you from playing big.

- What do I need to accept about my life right now, even if it's not where I want to be?

- What am I currently 'excusing' myself from? Be honest with yourself and write a list of all your excuses.

- What does the Think Like a Boss version of you look like?

- If £100,000 landed in your bank account tomorrow, what would you do with the money and why?

- What do you want your legacy to be?

- Write a love letter to yourself. This is one of the most empowering exercises you can do for yourself.

As you can see, journaling is a practice that offers countless benefits to your physical, mental, and emotional well-being. Whether it's a daily entry in a diary or reflections at weekends, journaling allows us to connect with ourselves, improve our self-awareness and embark on a journey of personal growth and discovery.

MORNING ROUTINE

How you start your day
sets the tone for the rest of your day.

We all have a morning routine. But whether your morning routine is helping you start your day the right way or hindering you, is a different question.

One routine that many people rave about is the '5 a.m. club.' This is a concept first introduced by writer and leadership expert Robin Sharma, who recommends waking up at 5 a.m. every day and dedicating the first hour of your morning to your personal growth and development. While there are plenty of benefits to waking up early, you don't need to wake up at 5 a.m. to have a productive day and win in life.

I'm not a member of the 5 a.m. club. In fact, the only time you'll see me awake at that time is if I'm catching an early morning flight or if I'm jet-lagged from crossing time zones. I am, however, an advocate of waking up early and making the most of my day. For me this means rising at 7 a.m., because it works best for me and my schedule. To instill habits that stick, find a routine that works for you. In an ideal world, try to wake up before the rest of your household and spend the first few minutes of your day setting your mind, body, and soul up for success, before life and society get in the way.

Creating a morning routine that works may take time; it may also require you to experiment a little. Here are a few tips to help you get started:

- **Don't start too big.** You're more likely to stick to a routine if it feels achievable, rather than if it feels constrained. Remember, life is a marathon not a sprint.

- **Set realistic goals.** Don't try to cram too much into your morning routine, especially when you first get started. Start with a few simple tasks that you can easily accomplish.

- **Be disciplined.** To begin with, set yourself a daily reminder to help you get into a consistent routine. The key is to stick to your routine as much as possible, even on weekends. Once you do something for long enough, it becomes ingrained and you'll be running on autopilot before long.

- **Have fun with it and try to make it enjoyable.** Your morning routine should be something you look forward to doing. The more enjoyable you make it, the more likely you are to stick to it.

- **Be flexible.** There will be days when your routine gets disrupted or needs to be modified. This is especially true for me when I'm traveling. Instead of starting my routine at 7 a.m., if I'm flying somewhere I'll do it several hours later. While I would have preferred to have done it much earlier, I still get it done because I know how much of a positive effect it has on my emotional well-being. As the saying goes... *better late than never!* If for any reason you don't manage to do your routine one day, don't let that discourage you – just return to it the next day.

An Example of My Morning Routine

- 7:00 a.m. Wake up and follow a guided meditation in bed for five minutes.

- 7:05 a.m. Listen to an uplifting song and do some deep breathing exercises.

- 7:10 a.m. Journal and do some visualization exercises.

- 7:30 a.m. Brush teeth, shower, dress, and drink some hot water and lemon.

- 7:50 a.m. Eat a healthy breakfast.

- 8:00 a.m. Leave house, go for a morning coffee, and get daily steps in.

- 9:00 a.m. Return home, check emails, respond to anything urgent, and start working on my most important task of the day.

While this routine works for me, it might not work for you. I've also been honing this routine for several years now, making tweaks along the way. I used to work out first thing in the morning, for example, but now I work out in the afternoon or evening, depending on the day. I do, however, always make sure that I get out in nature first thing in the morning, usually by walking to my local coffee shop and then through my favorite park. Remember, you're more likely to stick to a habit when you make it work for you.

Here's an example of another morning routine that you can adapt to your own needs:

- 6:00 a.m. Wake up, brush teeth, and drink a glass of water.

- 6:15 a.m. Meditate for five minutes.

- 6:20 a.m. Journal for 10 minutes.

- 6:30 a.m. Exercise for 20 minutes.

- 6:50 a.m. Shower and get dressed.

- 7:15 a.m. Eat a healthy breakfast.

- 7:45 a.m. Walk kids to school.

- 8:30 a.m. Check emails and respond to urgent messages.

- 8:45 a.m. Start working on the most important task of the day.

Plan your new morning routine – a powerful morning routine can change your life. When you start your day with intention and purpose, you're more likely to achieve your goals, reduce stress and anxiety, and live a more fulfilling life.

EVENING ROUTINE

A productive morning starts the night before...

I've introduced you to the concept of a morning routine; now let's look at evening routines. An evening routine is a set of activities that we do before bed and is arguably just as important as our morning routine. While morning actions set you up for the day, evening routines help you unwind, de-stress, and relax, promoting better sleep and helping you to prepare for the following day.

If you're not used to having an evening routine, it can be helpful to start small. Choose a few activities that you enjoy and that you can easily fit into your schedule. As you get used to your new lifestyle, you can add more activities, swap them out for other ones, or adjust the time you spend on each one.

Elements you might wish to incorporate into your bedtime routine include:

- **Activities that help you wind down**, such as having a warming bubble bath, listening to classical music, or reading a good book.

- **Reflecting on your day** and journaling on what went well, where can you improve, and what you're grateful for (*see Win Like a Boss Tip #8, p.209*).

- **Preparing for the next day.** This is your opportunity to get one step ahead and write your to-do list. You're then far less likely to get overwhelmed and far more likely to hit the ground running the next day because you know exactly what to work on.

Here are a few tips to help you get the most out of your evening routine:

- **Schedule a time every evening** to begin your bedtime routine and set a reminder if needed. This will help to make it a habit and gradually it will train your brain to naturally feel tired at bedtime and your body will get into a rhythm.

- **Create a relaxing environment.** As soon as it gets dark, dim the lights in your home. Light affects sleep more than any other external factor, even noise. Studies have shown that light exposure at night can disrupt the body's normal circadian rhythm – the internal body clock that controls your sleep/wake cycle. By dimming the lights, you're starting to get your body prepared for a restful state. Lighting a scented candle will provide a soft light as well as a calming aroma.

- **Avoid using screens** for at least one hour (ideally two hours) before bed. The blue light emitted from screens can interfere with sleep (*see How to Practice Good Sleep Hygiene, p.193*).

- **Be mindful of what you eat and drink before bed.** Try to avoid eating too late at night as this raises body temperature, impacting sleep onset – it can also impact the quality of your sleep.

- **Take this time to relax and de-stress.** This is your time to recharge your batteries and prepare for the next day.

- **Do activities that you enjoy.** Your evening routine should be something that you look forward to – if you don't enjoy an activity, you're less likely to stick with it.

An Example of My Evening Routine

- 8:00 p.m. Ensure all overhead lights at home are switched off apart from small lamps.

- 10:30 p.m. Light a scented candle in my bedroom or use a diffuser with essential oils.

- 10:35 p.m. Clean my teeth, wash my face, and get ready for bed.

- 10:40 p.m. Write my to-do list.

- 10:45 p.m. Spend five to 10 minutes reflecting on my day and gratitude journaling.

- 10:55 p.m. Meditate and visualize for three minutes.

- 10:58 p.m. Read a book for 10 to 15 minutes.

- 11:10 p.m. Listen to classical music or binaural beats as I fall asleep.

• • • • • •

While the topic of habits might not be the sexiest subject alive, I don't know of any successful or wealthy person who hasn't got to where they are without working on this area of their life in a conscious way. Remember: old habits don't open new doors!

PART VI

THE
MANIFESTO

LIVE LIKE A BOSS

The term 'Think Like a Boss' is so much more than an empowering statement. It's a way of being. One that will help you Think Big, Live Big, and Win Big in life. Here are some of my favorite principles that are guaranteed to upgrade your life in the best possible way. And the best news is – they're free!

MAKE PEOPLE FEEL GOOD IN YOUR PRESENCE

In my experience, one of the quickest ways to upgrade your life is by making people feel good in your presence. As humans, we all have an innate desire to feel seen, heard, and special. Whether you're having a good day or a bad day, the second someone makes you feel one (or more) of these three things, you instantly feel uplifted, lighter, and have more of a spring in your step. And being the person spreading these feel-good vibes feels amazing when you see what a difference it makes to people.

Here are three simple things you can do to spread some joy, really connect with people, and make them feel seen:

1. **Greet people with a smile** before any words are exchanged. Do this with everyone. Whether it's the host at a restaurant, the cleaner in the toilets, or the supermarket assistant at the checkout. This instantly makes people feel at ease and relaxed in your presence. You're also acknowledging them which makes them feel seen.

2. **Always start a conversation** with people. Especially if they're providing a service to you. A simple 'Hi, how are you today?' or 'Hi, how's your day going?' is enough. I can't tell you the number of times where the person on the receiving end of my question has thanked me for taking the time to acknowledge them and ask how they are. This is especially true of service staff, such as waiters, air stewards, bar staff, receptionists, and shop assistants. Sadly, some people look down on others, which can make them feel invisible or unimportant. It doesn't matter who you are or how rich you might be, you are never above anyone – ever. We are all humans who are worthy of respect.

3. **Pay people compliments.** I don't know one person on this planet who doesn't love to feel special and one of the most powerful ways you can do this is through paying people compliments. Whether it's, 'I love your hair'; 'what a pretty top you're wearing'; or 'you have great energy.' There's something special to appreciate about everyone, but how often do you notice these things and not say them out loud? Get into the habit of giving genuine compliments to the people you meet.

When you adopt this way of being, you'll experience greater connection with the people around you, which will feel wonderful, and the added bonus is that you'll also witness your life upgrade, as people will want to make you feel good right back.

IF YOU DON'T ASK, YOU DON'T GET!

How often do you accept things that are given to you – even if they're not quite what you want? If you're anything like I used to be, your answer is probably a lot. Whether it's a hotel room overlooking an alleyway, the worst table at a restaurant, or the middle seat on a plane. Most people live their lives accepting things because they're afraid to be honest about what they really want.

What if I told you that life doesn't have to be this way? What if I told you that you can have more and doing so will enrich your life in more ways than you can imagine? You get to raise the bar on what you're willing to accept. You also get to attract things that will add to your life, not take from it, just by changing your way of being. When you Think Like a Boss, you don't settle for what's handed to you, *you ask for what you know is available to you.*

One concept I live my life by and that I encourage the world to live by is: if you don't ask you don't get. When you embrace this idea, you don't just accept the first thing you're offered if you know that there is a better alternative available. Instead, you ask for more, knowing that in the worst-case scenario, you're in the exact same position that you started in, meaning you haven't lost anything.

In my experience, when you work up the courage to ask for what you really want, people will often go above and beyond to help you as far as they can. This is especially the case when you make them feel seen, heard, and special. Here are some things to try when working with this principle. I bet you'll be surprised by the results!

The next time you go to a restaurant and there's nothing you fancy on the menu, ask if the chefs can prepare you something else. Be specific about what you want though – people are more likely to accommodate your request if you make their life as easy as possible.

The next time you're at an airport check-in desk or at the gate to board a flight, ask the agent if there are any extra legroom seats or upgrades available. Feel free to go to town about why you would gratefully appreciate this option. One reason I regularly cite if I don't get my preferred seating on flights is that I'm tall and have long legs. It works every time!

The next time you check in to a hotel, ask for a beautiful room with a view, on a high floor (unless you have a thing about heights!). And if you're celebrating a special occasion, such as a birthday or anniversary, be sure to tell the receptionist or mention it when booking. I've lost count of the number of times I've received room upgrades, or complimentary cakes, chocolates, flowers, bottles of wine, prosecco, or champagne have made their way to my hotel room, because I shared the occasion I was celebrating!

The next time you arrive at a bar or a restaurant without a reservation (especially one where it's difficult to get a booking), ask the host if there are any last-minute cancellations. Or if you don't need the table for long, ask if there are any tables available where the reservation is scheduled for sometime later. Let them know that you are happy to vacate the table before the next guest arrives.

These are some small ways to start building your confidence about asking for what you really want. Once you become more comfortable with using this principle, then you can start to apply it to other areas of your life, such as asking your boss for a pay rise or a promotion. Again, you may be surprised by the results!

Remember – if you don't ask, the answer will always be 'no!'

YOU'RE NEVER TOO SMALL TO WIN BIG

Wherever you're at on your journey in life, know this: you're never too small to win big. The world is full of stories about people who've overcome the odds and achieved great things – especially underdogs. Here are a few examples to inspire you.

Sylvester Stallone

Imagine having to sell your dog for $40 in front of a 7-Eleven store, just to make ends meet. In the 1970s, before his big break, Sylvester Stallone did just that. Stallone was so broke that he couldn't even afford to buy food, so he sold his dog Butkus to survive.

After writing the *Rocky* script in three-and-a-half days, he was offered $360,000 for the screenplay on the condition that he wouldn't star in the film. Stallone stood his ground and refused to sell unless he could star as Rocky himself. He also only had $106 in his bank account at the time. Stallone's persistence and determination paid off. The movie became a hit and the film went on to win three Oscars. He later bought his dog back for $15,000 and said Butkus was worth every cent!

Emma Raducanu

In 2021, tennis player Emma Raducanu shocked the world and made history when she won the US Open and became the first ever qualifier to win a major tournament. Ranked outside the top 300 at the start of the year, Emma won the US Grand Slam at just 18 years old, beating Leylah Fernandez in the final. Before Raducanu, no qualifier in the open era, male or female, had ever reached a Grand Slam final. Emma was also the first British woman to win a Grand Slam in 44 years!

Leicester City

If you'd asked football fans at the start of the 2015-16 football season, which club they tipped as favorites to win the UK Premier League that year, the last team they would have predicted were underdogs Leicester City.

Prior to that season, the club had spent most of its footballing history in the lower divisions of English football. It had only been promoted to the Premier League in 2014 and the team's manager, who was new to the club in 2015, was seen as a relatively underwhelming appointment.

Leicester City's squad wasn't among the strongest in the league, nor did they have the financial resources to attract big-name players from top clubs such as Arsenal, Chelsea, Manchester United or Liverpool.

After narrowly avoiding relegation the previous year, bookmakers gave Leicester City odds of 5,000–1 to come top of the table. What's more, Kim Kardashian was given better odds of becoming the next US president than Leicester City was of winning the Premier League that year!

Much to everyone's amazement, and despite the odds being stacked against them, Leicester City lost just three matches that season, winning 23 in total. They were also 10 points clear at the top of the table when they were announced as the winners of the Premier League – with many claiming it as the most astonishing title win in football history.

The squad's success was fuelled by hard work and exceptional teamwork. They are also testament to the fact that even the most unexpected teams can achieve greatness!

YOU NEVER GET A SECOND CHANCE TO MAKE A GOOD FIRST IMPRESSION

Did you know that you have just a few seconds to make a good first impression? Even more interestingly, experiments conducted by researchers at Princeton University suggest that it takes only a tenth of a second to start making accurate judgments about people's traits.[1]

Now, one concept I live my life by is this: you never quite know who you're going to meet. Yes, we all have certain plans or routines that are set in stone and yes, our calendars and schedules might be planned out days, weeks, or even months in advance. But, as much as we try and control how our day goes, you just never quite know what might unfold, who you might meet, or what opportunities could present themselves at a moment's notice that may change your life forever.

With this concept in mind, how you show up and present yourself matters. From the words you speak, to the way you behave and interact with others. Be mindful of how you show up for yourself. Smile, be polite, empower yourself and others, feel good in what you're wearing, and, if you don't, then don't wear it. First impressions are formed very quickly and can be difficult to change.

PRINCIPLE #5

FIND A WAY OUT
OF NO WAY

I'm a firm believer that solutions exist for pretty much everything. When you adopt this mindset, you find a way out of 'no way' – even when it feels like the odds are stacked against you.

A good example occurred a few years ago, when the unthinkable happened after I boarded a train from Manchester to Liverpool. Or rather, I thought I had boarded a train from Manchester to Liverpool. The train I actually boarded, by mistake, was bound for London, making a two-and-a-half-hour journey in the wrong direction.

The train was 40 minutes into its journey when I heard the conductor announce that our next and final stop would be London Euston.

'London,' I repeated, with a confused look on my face. 'I don't understand....'

I'd been so preoccupied on my mobile phone until that point that I'd blocked out all announcements and hadn't once thought to check I was on the right train. Now in my defense, I was so accustomed to commuting between

Manchester and London at weekends (for a decade, when I worked in banking), that out of habit I'd gone to the platform that the London-bound train departed from and accidentally boarded the wrong train.

'F*ck!' I shouted, 'I'm on the wrong train!' I needed to be in Liverpool for a really important event.

No sooner had the panic set in when it dawned on me that firstly, I categorically couldn't miss the event in Liverpool that was starting in under two hours. Secondly, it would be a five-hour round-trip minimum, if I had to go to London and back. And thirdly, I didn't have a ticket for the London train, so I would need to pay the £250 penalty fare for boarding a train without a ticket.

I had to find a way to get off that train, even if the odds were stacked against me.

As I scrambled out of my seat to go and find the train manager and explain my situation, my brain kicked into overdrive. I anxiously played out all the different scenarios in my head and the only viable solution was to get off that train quickly, even though there were no more stops until London.

Looking back now, I can't even imagine how I came across when I eventually blurted out my story to the train manager. One thing for sure was clear – the sheer panic that was written all over my face. It was evident just by looking at me that I was telling the truth, even though my words didn't make much sense.

The last thing I recall saying to him, as he sat me down in his tiny office in carriage C before rushing off to make a few calls, was: 'Please help me... there has to be a way for me to get off this train, because I categorically have to be in Liverpool in 90 minutes' time.'

What happened next still blows me away, and makes me so thankful for the good-hearted people who exist in this world.

Just 15 minutes after my emotional outburst to the train manager, our train made an unscheduled stop and pulled up at Nuneaton. This station wasn't on the official route and no passengers were permitted to get on or off the train, with the exception of one person – me! What's more, as I disembarked the train, another high-speed train was waiting for me to board on the opposite platform – it was heading to Liverpool. The Liverpool-bound train also wasn't scheduled to stop at Nuneaton, but because the train manager had taken pity on me, he put a call out to all the drivers on his network to ask if any trains heading to Liverpool were willing to make a detour and stop at Nuneaton, to pick me up.

As I ran off one train and onto the next, I recall crying tears of gratitude as I waved to the train manager, thanking him profusely for helping me. By this point the whole train (which had several hundred people on board) had heard of my plight and waved me off as I shouted: 'Thank you, thank you, thank you,' on repeat. The best news is, I made it to Liverpool with a few minutes to spare, I didn't have to pay any penalties, and I received the most incredible service from both train managers. The Liverpool-bound train even had a drink ready for me, to calm my nerves.

It would have been so easy for me to accept the situation for what it was and to admit defeat, miss my event, pay the £250 penalty, and lose over five hours of my day. But that's not what we do when we Think Like a Boss. We find a way out of no way. Even when you think there's no solution, I promise you there always is!

YOU EITHER WIN OR YOU LEARN; YOU NEVER, EVER LOSE

This is a powerful way to see life and a great example of a growth mindset. When you take action, only one of two outcomes exist. You either win or you learn, you never, ever lose. You see, everything in life teaches us something. Our experiences either bring us closer to what we want, or they show us exactly what we don't want.

When you have taken an action of some sort, irrespective of what the outcome or result is, ask yourself the following powerful questions to support your growth:

- What went well?

- What contributed to the win/setback?

- Where can I improve?

- What would I do differently next time around (if anything)?

Every outcome, whether a victory or a setback, holds valuable lessons and by embracing this mindset, we gain even more knowledge, wisdom, and resilience: leading to more personal and professional success.

The gift is in your answers and the answers are in your reflections.

YOUR DIET ISN'T JUST WHAT YOU EAT

Pay attention to everything, because every thought you think and every action you take contribute to your current reality. If you're not living the life that you actually want, it's because you keep feeding the life that you don't really want. Now, read that statement again.

If you're not living the life that you actually want to live, it's because you keep feeding the life that you don't want to live. From the people you interact and surround yourself with, to your career opportunities, job prospects, relationship status, and health – your quality of life is directly influenced by what you feed yourself.

Things to think about include:

- **What you watch.** Notice the media you consume, including movies, TV shows, and social media. These can all significantly impact your thoughts, your emotions, and your behaviors. To Win Big, you have to Think Big and this means not exposing yourself to negative news or consuming content from people who aren't good role models, on repeat. Be mindful that what you watch will help to promote positive values and perspectives.

- **What you read.** Books, articles, and other forms of literature can do wonders for broadening your knowledge, inspiring you with ideas, and opening your eyes to a different perspective on life. Reading widely can also expand your understanding of the world, leading to a more positive outlook on life, and contributing to your personal growth in the process.

- **Who you follow.** The people you follow online, in your local communities, and in your professional networks can heavily influence your values, beliefs, and aspirations. Surrounding yourself with inspiring, like-minded, and supportive individuals can have a positive impact on your outlook and well-being.

- **Who you spend time with.** The company we keep plays a significant role in shaping our lives. Spending time with people who uplift, inspire, and support you can contribute to your happiness and success, whereas the opposite can be said when you associate with negative or unsupportive individuals.

As you can see, your 'diet' can have a profound impact on your physical, mental, and emotional health, *and of course* on your personal and professional success. If you're not yet living the life you want to live, now is the time to change that. The sooner you start making conscious choices to feed the life you want, the sooner your life will start to change.

TRUST THE NEXT CHAPTER BECAUSE YOU ARE THE AUTHOR

It's true. You are the author of your own life story. Not your parents, or your loved ones, or your mentors, or your employers. In the same way that you put your trust into others, such as the bus driver who drives the bus to work, or the teachers who look after your children at school – trust yourself.

This means owning your power, being honest about what you want, and taking control of your life.

Throughout my 20s and early 30s, I constantly gave my power away. To my employers mainly; working 70-hour weeks was the norm and on bad weeks it could stretch as high as 100 hours. I never challenged the work culture because I told myself that it was expected of me. I missed out on birthdays, weddings, and celebrations because I allowed my employers to control my diary. This meant I was often overseas for weeks on end (usually at a moment's notice), which caused a great deal of frustration, stress, and arguments with loved ones.

It got to the point where I'd lost my own inner compass and sense of knowing, because I was constantly seeking approval or running decisions past others, instead of doing what I thought was best.

This is why it took me as long as it did to leave the banking industry – I didn't trust myself enough to walk away from a career that I'd spent a decade building, to start a business from ground zero and make it work.

If I've learned anything from my own story, it's trust yourself. Because when push comes to shove, you will never let yourself down, especially if you have a compelling enough want or need, like we discussed in Part II of the book (see p.51). You will make things work because you have to make them work. When you have bills to pay and food to put on the table, you have no other option but to show the f*ck up for yourself.

Let this be your reminder today that you already have all the answers within you. If you need to take a little quiet time, to drown out the noise of other people's voices, to remember who you are and what you want: do it. Stand in your power of being the author of your own story, one chapter at a time.

IT'S ONLY EVER YOU VERSUS YOU

When it comes to comparing yourself to other people – don't. Nothing good comes from it, nor will it ever. All you're doing is setting yourself up for a fall, which can lead to feeling inadequate, not enough, disappointed, frustrated, triggered, and discouraged. Instead, I invite you to Think Like a Boss and make a like-for-like comparison – by comparing the current version of yourself with a more outdated version, instead of measuring yourself against other people.

The reason why you're the best possible benchmark to measure yourself against is because your view of other people is often distorted, especially when you throw social media into the mix – which is where the majority of people spend their time when they're online.

Remember, people only ever share what they want to share, and it's often a curated representation of their best moments and highlight reels, rather than an accurate reflection of their day-to-day reality.

When you adopt the mindset of 'it's only ever you versus you,' you can only win. Not only is it a great confidence-booster to see how far you've come and what you're capable of, but tracking your progress can also be a powerful incentive for staying focused and hitting your goals.

Remember, everyone is unique and has their own distinct path ahead of them, and when you strive to be better than you were yesterday, you're on the path to growth.

DON'T DIM YOUR LIGHT TO MAKE OTHER PEOPLE FEEL MORE COMFORTABLE

Nothing good comes from playing small, as I highlight throughout this book. Not only are you being inauthentic, but it can also be exhausting, as you're not allowing yourself to express who you truly are or who you desire to be. There's enough that's fake in this world, without you adding to it.

Instead, be you. And be completely unapologetic about it. You get to be extra and show off your extroverted personality, if that's who you are. Equally you get to work in silence and let success be your noise, if that aligns more with your personality.

Give yourself permission to shine brightly because wonderful things happen when you step into your greatness. You also model and inspire others to do the same.

DON'T TAKE ADVICE FROM PEOPLE WHO AREN'T WHERE YOU WANT TO BE

How many times have you asked someone for advice instead of listening to your own intuition only to revert back to your initial thoughts? The next time you seek answers from other people, remember this:

- **They might not have the experience or knowledge you're looking for.** If someone isn't already where you desire to be then they don't have the first-hand knowledge or experience to give you helpful advice. They might be relying on theory or second-hand information, which may not even be accurate or relevant to your question.

- **Their advice might be biased.** People who haven't accomplished what you're trying to do are more likely to recommend that you start by playing small. Their advice is likely to be based on their own fears and insecurities. As a result, they might discourage you from taking risks or pursuing your dreams because they don't want to see you fail.

- **They might not be able to relate to your situation.** If someone hasn't walked in your shoes, they might not be able to fully understand your challenges and aspirations. They may end up giving you advice that is not practical or relevant to your exact situation.

- **They may be triggered by you or feel threatened or jealous.** Be wary of taking advice from people who are threatened by you or jealous of you – not everyone will have achieved your level of success yet so they may try to sabotage you by giving you bad advice. They may even give you advice that is designed to hold you back and stop you reaching your full potential.

Instead of seeking advice from people who are not where you want to be:

- **Join a community of people** who are where you want to be and seek guidance from them.

- **Listen to your intuition.** It's your internal compass for navigating life. Your intuition also knows you better than anyone.

- **Think about your values and goals.** Make sure that whoever you're listening to for advice aligns with your personal values and long-term goals.

- **Trust your own judgment** and make the choices that feel right for you.

MOTIVATION GETS YOU GOING BUT DISCIPLINE KEEPS YOU GROWING

There's an inherent assumption that motivation alone is enough of an incentive to keep you on track to hit your goals. Sadly, this isn't the case. Motivation can be a great catalyst to kickstart you into action, but discipline is what keeps you developing and growing.

Think of it like this: motivation is what helps you do what needs to be done when you want to do it. Discipline is doing what needs to be done when you don't!

Motivation is something that comes and goes, it's a feeling rather than something you choose to do or that you can control. Whereas discipline is an action – it's something you do and choose to do.

Results depend on action, and the most effective way to consistently take action is by mastering the skill of self-discipline. Personally, I see self-discipline as a skill. A skill isn't something that we're born with; it's something we train ourselves to become good at over time. In the same way that you train to run a marathon, or you train yourself to lift weights, discipline is a skill that you can master over time and, once mastered, it becomes a habit and an integral factor for success.

Here's how to master self-discipline:

- **Create a roadmap or plan** of what you're aiming for as a starting point. Revert back to the goal-setting section in Part II of this book (*see p.79*), and use the exercises there. Remember, research has shown that people who write their goals or plans down are more likely to achieve them than those who don't.

- **Set an alarm** on your phone to remind you to do the thing that you're trying to build into a habit. I often find that the earlier in the day I do something, the less likely I'm to talk myself out of it, especially when I'm just beginning to form a new habit.

- **Habit stack.** Integrate the new activity into something that you're already doing where possible (*see p.170*).

- **Track your progress.** This can be a great motivator. Lots of times people only want to do the action once they see the results, but success doesn't work that way. You have to do the actions long before the results are visible.

- **Identify anything that could potentially throw you off your game.** Remove distractions or temptations. If your goal is to eat better, for example, throw away any unhealthy food in your cupboard.

- **Hold yourself accountable.** This could be in the form of a friend, a mentor, or even an app. I use a running app, for example, to track my runs and log all my times. This gives me a nice boost at the end of each run and incentivizes me to want to keep going.

- **Reward yourself when you hit key milestones.** It's always fun to celebrate yourself and it's something you should take great pleasure in and get comfortable with. You get to champion yourself for taking action toward your goals and toward becoming a happier, healthier, and more fulfilled version of yourself.

- **Have reminders lying around of what you know is possible.** I take screenshots of my desires and put them as the wallpaper on my phone. I also stick photos of a visual representation of the goals that I'm working toward on my fridge and on my office walls.

DON'T LET STARTING SMALL STOP YOU FROM THINKING BIG

Remember that miracle we spoke about, at the beginning of this book...? In case it wasn't clear already. You're never too small to think big. Ever. It doesn't matter who you are, where you come from, or what you do. If you can dream it and you see someone else doing it – you can do it too.

The people you see making things happen dreamt big. They found something they were interested in, they got good at it, and now they're winning. You don't need talent to succeed. Talent is a skill and a skill can be learned.

If anyone discourages you, with comments such as:

Why don't you be realistic?

What do you know about X?

Don't you think you have your head in the clouds?

I'm not sure that's practical.

Ignore them. People will tell you to be realistic, but realism only gets you so far. The magic comes in thinking big. When you allow your mind to think big thoughts, and you think these thoughts on a regular basis, you're anchoring your desires into your subconscious. As we know from previous chapters, your subconscious is where it's at. So, don't play small: think big. Put one foot in front of the other and keep moving.

DON'T RELY ON OTHER PEOPLE TO GIVE YOU WHAT YOU WANT

If you want something done and it's important to you – do it yourself. Is it nice to feel supported? Yes. Is it nice when people have your back? Of course. But no one will care about your goals or dreams the way you do.

If I waited every time someone promised to connect me with someone, invite me somewhere, or send me a link to something, I wouldn't have done half the things that I've done. People forget. Life gets busy and as I said, no one cares as much as you do.

Use your initiative. Be brave. Actively pursue what you want. If at first you don't succeed, find another way. You can never be let down when you rely on yourself.

'KEEP YOUR EYES ON THE STARS, AND YOUR FEET ON THE GROUND'

THEODORE ROOSEVELT

One of the best pieces of advice I've ever received is from my dear friend Niyc. Her motto in life is: *always be the student*. No matter who you are, what you do, who you know, or how long you've had skin in the game – you're never above anyone. Be humble. Stay grounded. Don't look down on people and above all, be open to learning from everybody.

Life is about finding balance, and you want to find that sweet spot. If you tip the scales too much on one side, the other side will be out of whack. It's also important to have a foundation from which to build while dreaming big and having aspirations. Being kind, humble, and treating people with respect will get you far, but if you don't believe the impossible is possible, it'll keep you playing small.

STAY IN YOUR LANE: THERE'S NO TRAFFIC IN YOUR LANE

If you want to be productive and have more time to dedicate to the things that are meaningful and important to you, focus on you and you alone. When you get distracted or side-tracked by other people, you're expending energy in the wrong direction.

By staying in your lane you:

- **Avoid comparison.** Comparing yourself to others can lead to feelings of inadequacy, self-doubt, and even resentment. This is less likely to happen when you stay in your lane.

- **Have more clarity and focus.** You also have a clearer sense of direction because you're not getting distracted or suffering from FOMO.

- **Get ahead quicker.** Your energy is on you and your goals. The more time and energy you invest in yourself, the further ahead you'll be.

If you're someone who gets easily distracted by others here are some tips:

- **Set clear goals and priorities for yourself.** You should know exactly what you're doing from the moment you wake, to the minute you go to sleep. Schedule everything.

- **Set reminders for all your tasks.** This will help you stay on track.

- **Turn your phone off or enable flight safe mode during working hours.** This will minimize distractions and avoid you reaching for your phone to internet scroll (*see Setting Yourself Up for Success, p.173*).

- **Limit your time on social media** – the world spends too much time as it is online. While social media is a key component of most people's lives and has its benefits, people have also become depressed and even committed suicide as a result of their screen obsession. Cutting down on your online time increases self-esteem and helps to prevent comparisons.

Remember, just because you see a colleague, a peer, or a friend doing something, doesn't mean it's right for you. What's right for one person isn't necessarily right for the next. Allow your intuition to guide you.

Lastly, staying in your lane doesn't mean isolating yourself or ignoring the world. It just means you know where your priorities lie. You also know that the only person who can move the needle forward in your life is you. Stay focused and let your own internal compass show you the way.

THE BIGGEST WAY TO KILL A DREAM IS TO INTRODUCE IT TO A SMALL MIND

Be careful who you share the inner workings of your mind and life with. The majority of the world plays small. People don't take action or they self-sabotage because they fear the unknown. They're also afraid to leave the safety of their comfort zone. What can then happen when you share a dream with someone is they may:

- put you down

- question your desires

- not react with the excitement you'd hoped for

This can then leave you feeling deflated and questioning yourself. It can also stop you moving forward, especially if you're surrounded by too many limiting influences.

The best piece of advice I can give you is: surround yourself with big minds and never stop. The crazier you dream, the better. There is no logic to big dreams and there shouldn't be. Desires stem from emotion not logic. If we only made decisions based on logic, it wouldn't lead to a very exciting life. Nor would it show us the power of manifestation and visualization.

Never stop learning or dreaming. Get in rooms with people who are already where you desire to be. They are all the proof you need that the same is possible for you too.

YOU ONLY LOSE WHEN YOU GIVE UP

If you ever need reminding of why you should keep going and never quit, even when it feels like you're being tested the most, meet Sean Swarner.[2] Aged just 13, Sean was taken to his local hospital to get checked out after injuring himself in a basketball game, only to be diagnosed with stage four Hodgkin lymphoma. Initially, Sean was given just three months to live, but miraculously, after undergoing 10 months of chemotherapy and gaining 60-70lbs (27-32kg) from the steroids he was required to take, Sean went into remission.

Two years later, Sean was diagnosed with a second form of cancer that was completely unrelated to the first – a form that affects just three out of one million people, and has a prognosis of a 6 percent survival rate. Doctors gave Sean just 14 days to live and the treatment was so harsh, they had to put him in a medically induced coma. Except for one month of radiation therapy, Sean doesn't remember being 16 years old.

Despite being given just 14 days to live, with his relentless will and determination, Sean beat his second cancer, Askin's tumor, but it took something from him – one of his lungs. In 2002, after beating both forms of cancer, Sean decided that he wanted to become a beacon of hope for everyone touched by cancer. He didn't want what he went through to define him, and his number-one goal was to inspire those touched by the disease and scream hope from the highest platform he could find.

Initially, Sean wanted to climb Mount Everest and be the first cancer survivor to do so, but then he got bitten by the climbing bug and decided, 'there are seven other continents, why not climb the highest mountain on each continent?' Climbing the highest mountain on each continent is called the Seven Summits, but if you include the North and South Poles too, it's known as the Explorer's Grand Slam.

Sean is the world's first and only two-times cancer survivor to complete the Explorer's Grand Slam – scaling the highest point on all seven continents and then hiking to the North and South Poles. Only a handful of people have ever achieved this, but no one against the overwhelming odds Sean faced, with just one lung! Sean is an incredible source of inspiration not only to other cancer survivors, but also to anyone who wants to overcome the odds.

When you set your mind on something and you get there, it tells someone who may also be struggling with something that they can develop the strength and resilience to beat the odds and accomplish their goals too.

REJECTION IS JUST A FORM OF REDIRECTION

Some of the world's greatest success stories have stemmed from receiving rejection after rejection. One of my favorite stories is that of Collette Divitto. Collette was born with Down syndrome and for a long time, she just wanted a job, a place where she could use her skills and be part of a team. But interview after interview, Collette kept hearing 'no' and was told that she was 'not a good fit.'

Collette knew she had something special to offer and refused to give up, despite 'no' after 'no.' After years of employment rejections and applying for every job going, Collette took matters into her own hands and, through courage and determination, started her own business. Collette infused her love for baking into a business venture, which is how Collettey's Cookies was born.

Collette runs all aspects of her business and ships her cookies all over the US and Canada. When she's not managing her 15 employees, Collette is also a disability activist, Tedx speaker, mentor, author, TV personality, and disruptor. She is laser focused on creating jobs for people with disabilities and inspires others to pursue their dreams despite the challenges they face. Her mission is to show everyone that people with disabilities can do amazing things. They just need a chance!

PRINCIPLE #20

TO LOSE PATIENCE IS TO LOSE THE BATTLE

Life is a marathon not a sprint, so if you want to do anything great, you have to learn the art of patience. One individual who has learned the power of patience from a young age is Hansel Enmanuel.

Hansel is a US college basketball player who lost one of his arms in a childhood accident. He was just six years old when a pile of cinder blocks fell on him and hurt him so badly that doctors had to amputate his left arm. At the time, he remembers thinking: 'what am I going to do now!?... It's over for me.'[3] But against the odds, Enmanuel found basketball and became an accomplished dunker.

Hansel moved from his home in the Dominican Republic to Florida aged 16, speaking almost no English, and made a name for himself playing basketball in high school, scoring prolifically against opponents who had use of all of their limbs. Colleges became interested in recruiting Enmanuel to their team after social media users published videos highlighting his skills and biggest plays. Initially, critics thought he played as a gimmick and didn't know if he could do it against top talent. He became known as the one-armed hooper and signed with Louisiana's Northwestern State University before signing with the Austin Peay Governors team.

'One important lesson that I have learned in my life as a student-athlete is the value of patience,' Enmanuel wrote in a statement shared on his Instagram account that continued:

> *'Success cannot be achieved overnight,*
> *and it is common to experience frustration*
> *and disappointment along the way.*
>
> *Sometimes, we may feel entitled to something*
> *we desire and have worked hard for, only to*
> *realize that we are not ready to receive it at*
> *the moment. However, through patience,*
> *we can persevere and reach our goals.'*[4]

Referring to his transfer stage in basketball, Enmanuel continued: 'As I enter the transfer portal, I am reminded of the power of patience. I am willing to wait and trust the process, even if it means waiting an entire season to achieve my goals.'

He confidently told the Associated Press in an interview: 'We're going to make it to the NBA. That's the big goal.'[5]

FINAL WORDS

Over the course of this book, I've introduced you to what it truly means to Think Like a Boss. A mindset that drives a new way of thinking and one that encourages a new way of being. The concepts I share throughout this book are so powerful that when you incorporate them into your day-to-day consistently, they will inevitably change your life for the better. From the thoughts that you think, to the people and opportunities you attract, nothing is off limits when you Think Like a Boss.

Lastly, should you need one final reminder...

You *get to show others* what's possible.

Don't let starting small stop you from thinking big.

Life gets to work out better than you expected, because you keep your eyes on the stars and your feet on the ground.

You find a way out of no way.

You trust the next chapter because you are the author.

You're okay with being underestimated.

You either win or you learn, you never, ever lose.

You don't dim your light for others.

Nor do you settle for things that don't light you up.

You get to win when you are the underdog, because you're never too small to win big.

You empower yourself always, because when you do, you're halfway there!

And if you're ever in doubt, always ask yourself the following question:

If I was thinking like a boss right now, what would I do, what words would I say, and what actions would I take?

Then start by taking actions that align with your response.

To your success!

Maggie xx

ENDNOTES

Part I

1. Gervis, Z. (2020), 'This is How Many Excuses the Average American Makes Every Day': nypost.com/2020/05/18/the-average-american-makes-this-many-excuses-every-day/ [Accessed 19 August 2024]

2. swns digital. (2022), 'The Typical Brit Makes Five Excuses a Day to Get Out of Doing Things – with "I'm Too Tired" the Most Common, According to Research': swnsdigital.com/uk/2022/01/the-typical-brit-makes-five-excuses-a-day-to-get-out-of-doing-things-with-im-too-tired-the-most-common-according-to-research/ [Accessed 19 August 2024]

3. Mikhail, A. (2023), 'This 102-Year-Old Shares Her Secrets to Aging with Grace: 3,800 Steps, an Adult Tricycle, and a Lot of Laughter,' *Fortune Well*: fortune.com/well/2023/04/08/aging-longevity-tips-102-year-old-gladys-mcgarey/ [Accessed 19 August 2024]

4. Huffington, A (2021): www.linkedin.com/pulse/we-can-build-our-dreams-any-age-arianna-huffington/ [Accessed 19 August 2024]

5. 'Social Comparison Theory', *Psychology Today*: www.psychologytoday.com/gb/basics/social-comparison-theory [Accessed 19 August 2024]

6. Anderer, J. (2023), 'Average Person Loses 26 Days Each Year to Wasted Time,' *StudyFinds*: studyfinds.org/loses-26-days-wasted-time/ [Accessed 19 August 2024]

7. Kemp, S. (2024), 'The Time we Spend on Social Media', *DataReportal*: bit.ly/4dtXNX1 [Accessed 19 August 2024]

8.   Karl, B. (2002), 'One of the Top Fears Among Americans,'
     Medium: medium.com/illumination-curated/the-number-one-
     fear-among-americans-3f89acfeed41 [Accessed
     19 August 2024]

9.   Lener, M. and Fifield, S. (2022), 'Freeing Yourself from the
     Imposter Within,' *Psychology Today*: www.psychologytoday.
     com/gb/blog/biopsychosocial-solution/202210/freeing-
     yourself-the-imposter-within [Accessed 19 August 2024]

10. Ericsson, K.A., et al. (1993), 'The Role of Deliberate Practice in
     the Acquisition of Expert Performance,' *Psychological Review*,
     100(3): 363–406: doi.org/10.1037/0033-295X.100.3.363
     [Accessed 19 August 2024]

Part II

1.   Forbes Profile. (2022), 'Leonardo Del Vecchio & Family,' *Forbes*:
     www.forbes.com/profile/leonardo-del-vecchio/#3c916dc673dc
     [Accessed 19 August 2024]

2.   American Psychiatric Association (2023), 'Purpose in Life Can
     Lead to Less Stress, Better Mental Well-being,' Psychiatry.org:
     www.psychiatry.org/News-room/APA-Blogs/Purpose-in-Life-
     Less-Stress-Better-Mental-Health [Accessed 19 August 2024]

3.   Shiba, K., et al. (2021), 'Higher Sense of Purpose May Be
     Linked to Lower Rate of Mortality, Study Finds', *Science Daily*:
     www.sciencedaily.com/releases/2022/11/221115184500.htm
     [Accessed 19 August 2024]

4.   Seligman, M. (2012). *Flourish: A Visionary New Understanding of
     Happiness and Well-Being*. New York: Atria.

5.   Cohn, M.A., et al. (2009), 'Happiness Unpacked: Positive
     Emotions Increase Life Satisfaction by Building Resilience,'
     Emotion, 9(3): 361–368: psycnet.apa.org/doiLanding?doi=10.10
     37%2Fa0015952 [Accessed 19 August 2024]

6.   Oppland, M. (2016), '8 Traits of Flow According to Mihaly
     Csikszentmihalyi': positivepsychology.com/mihaly-
     csikszentmihalyi-father-of-flow/ [Accessed 19 August 2024]

7.   Umberson D. and Montez J.K., (2010), 'Social Relationships
     and Health: A Flashpoint for Health Policy,' *Journal of Health
     and Social Behavior*, 51 Supplement: s54–66: www.ncbi.nlm.nih.
     gov/pmc/articles/PMC3150158/ [Accessed 19 August 2024]

8. Pezirkianidis, C., et al. (2023), 'Adult Friendship and Wellbeing: A Systematic Review with Practical Implications,' *Frontiers in Psychology*, 24(14): www.frontiersin.org/journals/psychology/articles/10.3389/fpsyg.2023.1059057/full [Accessed 19 August 2024]

9. Abrams, Z. (2023), 'The Science of Why Friendships Keep us Healthy,' *American Psychological Association*, 54(4): www.apa.org/monitor/2023/06/cover-story-science-friendship [Accessed 19 August 2024]

10. Piat, M., et al. (2011), '"Who Believes Most in Me and in My Recovery": The Importance of Families for Persons with Serious Mental Illness Living in Structured Community Housing,' *Journal of Social Work in Disability & Rehabilitation*, 10(1): 49–65: www.ncbi.nlm.nih.gov/pmc/articles/PMC4835237/ [Accessed 19 August 2024]

11. Ong, H.S., et al. (2021), 'Family Engagement as Part of Managing Patients With Mental Illness in Primary Care,' *Singapore Medical Journal*, 62(5): 213–219: www.ncbi.nlm.nih.gov/pmc/articles/PMC8801858/ [Accessed 19 August 2024]

12. Clifton, J. (2022), 'The Power of Work Friends,' *Harvard Business Review*: hbr.org/2022/10/the-power-of-work-friends [Accessed 19 August 2024]

13. Berman, R. (2022), 'Having a Sense of Purpose May Help You Live Longer, Research Shows,' *Medical News Today*: www.medicalnewstoday.com/articles/longevity-having-a-purpose-may-help-you-live-longer-healthier [Accessed 19 August 2024]

14. Dictionary.com, Goal: www.dictionary.com/browse/goal [Accessed 19 August 2024]

15. Locke, E.A., et al. (1981), 'Goal Setting and Task Performance: 1969–1980,' *Psychological Bulletin*, 90(1): 125–152: psycnet.apa.org/record/1981-27276-001 [Accessed 19 August 2024]

16. Rozen, M. (2023), 'How Committed Are You to Your New Year Goals?: A Quantitative Study on the Connection of Commitment and Performance with New Year Resolutions,' *Open Journal of Social Sciences*, 11: 415–428: www.scirp.org/journal/paperinformation?paperid=127789 [Accessed 19 August 2024]

17. Matthews, G. (2007), 'The Impact of Commitment, Accountability, and Written Goals on Goal Achievement,' *Psychology Faculty Presentations at Dominican Scholar*, 3:

scholar.dominican.edu/psychology-faculty-conference-presentations/3 [Accessed 19 August 2024]

18. Locke, E.A., et al. (1981), 'Goal Setting and Task Performance: 1969–1980,' *Psychological Bulletin*, 90(1): 125–152: psycnet.apa.org/record/1981-27276-001 [Accessed 19 August 2024]

19. Schippers, M.C. and Ziegler, N. (2019), 'Life Crafting as a Way to Find Purpose and Meaning in Life,' *Frontiers in Psychology*, 10: 2778: www.ncbi.nlm.nih.gov/pmc/articles/PMC6923189/ [Accessed 19 August 2024]

20. King, L. (2001), 'The Health Benefits of Writing about Life Goals,' *Personality and Social Psychology Bulletin*, 27: 798-807: www.researchgate.net/publication/247895325_The_Health_Benefits_of_Writing_about_Life_Goals [Accessed 19 August 2024]

21. Latham, G.P. and Locke, E.A. (1991), 'Self-Regulation Through Goal Setting,' *Organizational Behavior and Human Decision Processes*, 50(2): 212–247: www.sciencedirect.com/science/article/abs/pii/074959789190021K [Accessed 19 August 2024]

Part III

1. Covington, M.V. and Beery, R.G. (1976), *Self-Worth and School Learning* (The Principles of Educational Psychology Series): Thomson Learning.

2. Neff, K.D. (2009), 'The Role of Self-Compassion in Development: A Healthier Way to Relate to Oneself,' *Human Development*, 52(4): 211–214: www.ncbi.nlm.nih.gov/pmc/articles/PMC2790748/ [Accessed 19 August 2024]

3. Neff, K.D (2024) 'Self-Compassion': self-compassion.org/blog/the-physiology-of-self-compassion/ [Accessed 19 August 2024]

4. Neff, K.D. (2009), op. cit.

Part IV

1. Tseng, J. and Poppenk, J. (2020), 'Brain Meta-State Transitions Demarcate Thoughts Across task Contexts Exposing the Mental Noise of Trait Neuroticism,' *Nature Communications*, 11: 3480: www.nature.com/articles/s41467-020-17255-9 [Accessed 19 August 2024]

2. Otaosese (2020), 'Mind Is...': medium.com/@otaosese/this-is-how-powerful-your-mind-is-424615e568c9 [Accessed 19 August 2024]

3. The Reach Approach, 'The Four Aspects of the Mind': www.thereachapproach.co.uk/2018/05/25/the-four-aspects-of-the-mind-2/ [Accessed 04 September 2024]

4. Lee, H.A., et al. (2024), 'Effect of Dynamic Binaural Beats on Sleep Quality: A Proof-of-Concept Study with Questionnaire and Biosignals,' *Sleep*, Apr 17: zsae097: pubmed.ncbi.nlm.nih.gov/38629490/ [Accessed 19 August 2024]

5. Thriving Center of Psychology (2022), 'Which Generation Struggles to Set Healthy Boundaries the Most?': thrivingcenterofpsych.com/blog/setting-healthy-boundaries/ [Accessed 19 August 2024]

6. Smith, M. (2023), 'People-Pleasers Are at a Higher Risk of Burnout, says Harvard-Trained Psychologist – How to Spot the Signs,' CNBC Make it: www.cnbc.com/2023/05/21/harvard-trained-psychologist-people-pleasers-are-at-higher-risk-for-burnout.htm [Accessed 19 August 2024] I

7. Dictionary.com, Doomscrolling: www.dictionary.com/browse/doomscrolling [Accessed 19 August 2024]

8. Holman, A. E., et al. (2013), 'Media's Role in Broadcasting Acute Stress Following the Boston Marathon Bombings,' *PNAS*, 111(1): 93–98: www.pnas.org/doi/full/10.1073/pnas.1316265110 [Accessed 19 August 2024]

9. Blades R. (2021),'Protecting the Brain Against Bad News,' *CMAJ*, 193(12): E428–E429: www.ncbi.nlm.nih.gov/pmc/articles/PMC8096381/ [Accessed 19 August 2024]

10. Robertson C.E., et al. (2023), 'Negativity Drives Online News Consumption,' *Nature Human Behavior*, 7(5): 812–822: pubmed.ncbi.nlm.nih.gov/36928780/ [Accessed 19 August 2024]

11. Johnston, W.M. and Davey, G.C.L. (2011), 'The Psychological Impact of Negative TV News Bulletins: The Catastrophizing of Personal Worries,' *British Journal of Psychology*, 88(1): 85–91: bpspsychub.onlinelibrary.wiley.com/doi/10.1111/j.2044-8295.1997.tb02622.x [Accessed 19 August 2024]

12. Mohammadi, N., et al. (2018), 'A Randomized Trial of an Optimism Training Intervention in Patients with Heart Disease,' *General Hospital Psychiatry*, 51: 46–53:

www.sciencedirect.com/science/article/abs/pii/
S016383431730439 [Accessed 19 August 2024]

13. Statista (2024), 'Number of Internet and Social Media Users Worldwide as of April 2024': www.statista.com/statistics/617136/digital-population-worldwide/ [Accessed 19 August 2024]

14. Kemp, S. (2024), 'The Time we Spend on Social Media,' *DataReportal*: datareportal.com/reports/digital-2024-deep-dive-the-time-we-spend-on-social-media [Accessed 19 August 2024]

15. Longstreet, P. and Brooks, S. (2017), 'Life Satisfaction: A Key to Managing Internet & Social Media Addiction,' *Technology in Society*, 50: 73–77: www.sciencedirect.com/science/article/abs/pii/S0160791X16301634 [Accessed 19 August 2024]

16. Rothwell, J. (2023), 'Teens Spend Average of 4.8 Hours on Social Media Per Day,' *Gallup*: news.gallup.com/poll/512576/teens-spend-average-hours-social-media-per-day.aspx [Accessed 19 August 2024]

17. Rothwell, J. (2023), 'How Parenting and Self-Control Mediate the Link Between Social Media Use and Youth Mental Health,' *Institute for Family Studies and Gallup*: ifstudies.org/ifs-admin/resources/briefs/ifs-gallup-parentingsocialmediascreentime-october2023-1.pdf [Accessed 19 August 2024]

18. Ibid. p.7

Part V

1. Palmer, C. (2020), 'Harnessing the Power of Habits,' *Monitor on Psychology*, 51(8): 78: www.apa.org/monitor/2020/11/career-lab-habits [Accessed 19 August 2024]

2. Wood, W., et al. (2002), 'Habits in Everyday Life: Thought, Emotion, and Action,' *Journal of Personality and Social Psychology*, 83(6): 1281–1297: psycnet.apa.org/doiLanding?doi=10.1037%2F0022-3514.83.6.1281 [Accessed 19 August 2024]

3. Contie, V. (2012), 'Old Habits Gone But Not Forgotten,' *NIH Research Matters*: www.nih.gov/news-events/nih-research-matters/old-habits-gone-not-forgotten [Accessed 19 August 2024]

4. Clear, J.: jamesclear.com/new-habit [Accessed 19 August 2024]

5. Duhigg, C. (2013), *The Power of Habit : Why We Do What We Do and How to Change*. p19. New York. Random House Books.

6. Chaney, S. (2023), 'Why You Shouldn't Check Your Phone When You Wake Up': www.makeuseof.com/you-shouldnt-check-phone-wake-up/ [Accessed 19 August 2024]

7. Robison, J. (2006), 'Too Many Interruptions at Work?' *Gallup*: news.gallup.com/businessjournal/23146/too-many-interruptions-work.aspx [Accessed 19 August 2024]

8. Ward, A.F., et al. (2017), 'Brain Drain: The Mere Presence of One's Own Smartphone Reduces Available Cognitive Capacity,' *Journal of the Association for Consumer Research*, 2(2): www.journals.uchicago.edu/doi/10.1086/691462 [Accessed 19 August 2024]

9. Kerai, A. (2023), 'Cell Phone Usage Statistics: Mornings Are for Notifications': www.reviews.org/mobile/cell-phone-addiction/ [Accessed 19 August 2024]

10. Bohlmeijer, E.T., et al. (2021), 'Promoting Gratitude as a Resource for Sustainable Mental Health: Results of a 3-Armed Randomized Controlled Trial up to 6 Months Follow-up,' *Journal of Happiness Studies*, 22: 1011–1032: link.springer.com/article/10.1007/s10902-020-00261-5 [Accessed 19 August 2024]

11. Iodice, J.A., et al. (2021), 'The Association Between Gratitude and Depression: A Meta-Analysis,' *International Journal of Depression & Anxiety*, 4: 024: clinmedjournals.org/articles/ijda/international-journal-of-depression-and-anxiety-ijda-4-024.php?jid=ijd [Accessed 19 August 2024]

12. Redwine L.S., et al. (2016), 'Pilot Randomized Study of a Gratitude Journaling Intervention on Heart Rate Variability and Inflammatory Biomarkers in Patients with Stage B Heart Failure,' *Psychosomatic Medicine*, 78(6): 667–676: www.ncbi.nlm.nih.gov/pmc/articles/PMC4927423/ [Accessed 19 August 2024]

13. Hazlett, L.I., et al. (2021), 'Exploring Neural Mechanisms of the Health Benefits of Gratitude in Women: A Randomized Controlled Trial,' *Brain, Behavior, and Immunity*, 95: 444–453: www.sciencedirect.com/science/article/pii/S088915912100177X [Accessed 19 August 2024]

14. Makhoul, M. and Bartley, E.J. (2023), 'Exploring the Relationship Between Gratitude and Depression Among Older

Adults with Chronic Low Back Pain: A Sequential Mediation Analysis,' *Front Pain Res (Lausanne)*, 4:1140778: www.ncbi.nlm. nih.gov/pmc/articles/PMC10196463/ [Accessed 19 August 2024]

15. Chattu, V.K., et al. (2019), 'The Global Problem of Insufficient Sleep and Its Serious Public Health Implications,' *Healthcare (Basel)*, 7(1): 1: www.ncbi.nlm.nih.gov/pmc/articles/ PMC6473877/ [Accessed 19 August 2024]

16. Vaccaro, A. and Dor, Y.K. (2020) 'Why Severe Sleep Deprivation Can be Lethal': brain.harvard.edu/hbi_news/why-severe-sleep-deprivation-can-be-lethal/ [Accessed 19 August 2024]

17. Potter, G.D.M., et al. (2017), 'Longer Sleep Is Associated with Lower BMI and Favorable Metabolic Profiles in UK adults: Findings from the National Diet and Nutrition Survey,' *PLOS ONE*, 12(7): journals.plos.org/plosone/article?id=10.1371/journal. pone.0182195 [Accessed 19 August 2024]

18. 'Sleep Deprivation May Cause People to Eat More Calories' (2016), *NeuroscienceNews*: neurosciencenews.com/caloric-intake-sleep-deprivation-5412/ [Accessed 19 August 2024]

19. 'Good Sleep for Good Health: Get the Rest You Need' (2021), *NIH News in Health*: newsinhealth.nih.gov/2021/04/good-sleep-good-health [Accessed 19 August 2024]

20. National Heart, Lung, and Blood Institute, 'How Sleep Affects Your Health': www.nhlbi.nih.gov/health/sleep-deprivation/ health-effects [Accessed 19 August 2024]

21. Nota, J.A. and Coles, M.E. (2018), 'Shorter Sleep Duration and Longer Sleep Onset Latency are Related to Difficulty Disengaging Attention from Negative Emotional Images in Individuals with Elevated Transdiagnostic Repetitive Negative Thinking,' *Journal of Behavior Therapy and Experimental Psychiatry*, 58: 114–122: www.sciencedirect.com/science/article/ abs/pii/S0005791617300629?via%3Dihub [Accessed 19 August 2024]

22. Goyal, M., et al. (2014), 'Meditation Programs for Psychological Stress and Well-being: A Systematic Review and Meta-analysis,' *JAMA Internal Medicine*, 174(3): 357–368: jamanetwork.com/journals/jamainternalmedicine/ fullarticle/1809754 [Accessed 19 August 2024]

23. Bostock, S., et al. (2019), 'Mindfulness On-The-Go: Effects of a Mindfulness Meditation App On Work Stress And Well-Being,'

Journal of Occupational Health Psychology, 24(1): 127–138: psycnet.apa.org/doiLanding?doi=10.1037%2Focp0000118 [Accessed 19 August 2024]

24. Kirk, U., et al. (2019), 'On-the-Spot Binaural Beats and Mindfulness Reduces Behavioral Markers of Mind Wandering,' *Journal of Cognitive Enhancement*, 3: 186–192: link.springer.com/article/10.1007/s41465-018-0114-z [Accessed 19 August 2024]

25. Bennike, I.H., et al. (2017), 'Online-Based Mindfulness Training Reduces Behavioral Markers of Mind Wandering,' *Journal of Cognitive Enhancement*, 1: 172–181: link.springer.com/article/10.1007/s41465-017-0020-9 [Accessed 19 August 2024]

26. Lindsay, E.K., et al. (2019), 'Mindfulness Training Reduces Loneliness and Increases Social Contact in a Randomized Controlled Trial,' *Proceedings of the National Academy of Sciences of the USA*, 116(9): 3488–3493: www.ncbi.nlm.nih.gov/pmc/articles/PMC6397548/ [Accessed 19 August 2024]

27. Bostock, S., et al., op. cit.

28. https://en.wikipedia.org/wiki/ [Accessed 19 August 2024]

29. Rusch, H.L., et al. (2019), 'The Effect of Mindfulness Meditation On Sleep Quality: A Systematic Review and Meta-Analysis of Randomized Controlled Trials,' *Annals of the New York Academy of Sciences*, 1445(1): 5–16: www.ncbi.nlm.nih.gov/pmc/articles/PMC6557693/ [Accessed 19 August 2024]

30. Jacka, F.N., et al. (2017), 'A Randomised Controlled Trial of Dietary Improvement for Adults with Major Depression (the 'SMILES' trial),' *BMC Medicine*, 15(23): bmcmedicine.biomedcentral.com/articles/10.1186/s12916-017-0791-y [Accessed 19 August 2024]

31. Cancer Research UK (2022), 'Can Cancer Be Prevented?': www.cancerresearchuk.org/about-cancer/causes-of-cancer/can-cancer-be-prevented-0 [Accessed 19 August 2024]

32. Noetel, M., et al. (2024), 'Effect of Exercise for Depression: Systematic Review and Network Meta-Analysis of Randomised Controlled Trials,' *BMJ*, 384:e075847: www.bmj.com/content/384/bmj-2023-075847 [Accessed 19 August 2024]

33. NHS Business Services Authority (2023), 'NHS Releases Mental Health Medicines Statistics for 2022/2023 in England': media.nhsbsa.nhs.uk/news/nhs-releases-mental-health-

medicines-statistics-for-20222023-in-england [Accessed 19 August 2024]

34. Attwell, C., et al. (2022), 'Cost of Living and Depression in Adults, Great Britain,' *Office for National Statistics*: www.ons. gov.uk/peoplepopulationandcommunity/healthandsocialcare/ mentalhealth/articles/costoflivinganddepressioninadults greatbritain/29septemberto23october2022 [Accessed 19 August 2024]

35. NHS, 'Exercise for Depression': www.nhs.uk/mental-health/ self-help/guides-tools-and-activities/exercise-for-depression/ [Accessed 19 August 2024].

36. Smyth, J.M., et al. (2018), 'Online Positive Affect Journaling in the Improvement of Mental Distress and Well-Being in General Medical Patients with Elevated Anxiety Symptoms: A Preliminary Randomized Controlled Trial,' *JMIR Mental Health*, 5(4): e11290: www.ncbi.nlm.nih.gov/pmc/articles/ PMC6305886/ [Accessed 19 August 2024]

Part VI

1. Willis, J. and Todorov, A. (2006), 'First Impressions: Making Up Your Mind After a 100-Ms Exposure to a Face,' *Psychological Science*, 17(7): 592–598: journals.sagepub.com/doi/10.1111/ j.1467-9280.2006.01750.x [Accessed 19 August 2024]

2. *True North: The Sean Swarner Story* (2017), Amazon: www. amazon.com/True-North-Sean-Swarner-Story/dp/ B07LBCSFCD [Accessed 19 August 2024].

3. Goh, Z.K. (2023), 'The Inspirational Story of Hansel Enmanuel, the One-Armed D1 College Basketball Player': olympics.com/ en/news/hansel-enmanuel-d1-college-basketball [Accessed 19 August 2024]

4. @enmanuelhansel. (20 March 2023). www.instagram.com/p/ CqBPXxROo8S/?utm_source=ig_web_button_share_ sheet&img_index=2 [Accessed 19 August 2024]

5. Goh, Z.K. op. cit.

ACKNOWLEDGMENTS

In loving memory of my dear Uncle Stuart, who read more books than anyone I know. Thank you for guiding me from above. I miss you every day.

To my publisher Hay House, thank you for believing in me and my legacy. With special thanks to Amy Kiberd, Cathy Levy and Louise Tucker.

Dad, thank you for being my biggest inspiration and my hero. Watching you survive C when the odds were stacked against you, was instrumental in me developing my Think Like a Boss mindset. Mum, you are the strongest woman I know – thank you for being my greatest role model. I love you both dearly!

To Ian, from the bottom of my heart, thank you. You've facilitated so much of this journey and this book wouldn't have been possible without you.

To Lucy, thank you for being such a dear friend and for being the greatest protector I could wish for. How you do what you do I'll never know but I am and forever will remain in your deepest gratitude.

To Andy, thank you for taking your proofing responsibilities so seriously. I will never forget dashing to your local wine bar in Spain because the Wifi stopped working just before my final edit was due. Seriously though, Wifi and wine... what more could an author ask for the night before a deadline!

To my soul sisters, Alex, Amber, Carmen, Caroline, Dawn, Jeanette, Lauren, Mel, and Niyc – thank you for being on this crazy journey with me and for constantly reminding me that I was born to do this. Your consistent source of love, light, friendship, protection, and strength, is something I will cherish forever. I love you all dearly.

To Laura and Vicky – what a ride! Who could have predicted the unfolding of everything. Thank you for the laughs, the cries, the support, and everything in between. Love you both!

To Frank, Jackie and Lin, thank you for your support and inspiration.

To Benny, Fadi, Gustavo and Rich, thank you for your friendship and for continuously checking-in and cheering me on. I'm so grateful to have you in my life!

To Gav, Izzy, Michael, Molly, Paige, Paulina, Ruby, and Will – thank you for fueling me with coffee and cake nearly every day for eight months! Just Between Friends not only serves the best coffee in the world, but it also has the best baristas. Our daily chats kept me going more than you'll ever know and I'm so grateful to you all!

To Dr C, thank you for peering at my laptop screen at JBF and then asking me if I was writing a book, too. I have admired your work for years. Your advice and words of wisdom were exactly what I needed to hear that day and every time I have even the slightest wobble, I come back to what you said. Thank you and I can't wait to read your new book!

To the little people in my life – Alex, Ava, Charlotte, Hallie Drew, Heidi, and Leo. Your innocence and child-like magic are such a joy to watch. You're evolving into the most remarkable children. Never stop believing in yourselves or in the power of magic!

Lastly, to you, my dear reader. Thank you for being my 'why'. The reason why I do what I do. Thank you for reminding me daily, why the work that I do matters and if you're ever experiencing even the smallest seed of doubt, come back to this book. I will always be here to motivate you, empower you, and cheer you all the way to the finish line!

Lola Miche Photography

ABOUT THE AUTHOR

Maggie Colette is a certified positive psychology coach, motivational speaker, author, and has a top 2 percent global-ranking podcast. After more than 10 years scaling the heights of the private banking world, she quit to pursue her dream and embark on her biggest mission to date – to empower the world to believe that they can. Now she helps people elevate their mindset and unleash their potential.

Maggie reaches over 70 million people worldwide every month through Think Like a Boss® – an online platform she created in 2018, dedicated to mindset, motivation, and success. She's also mentored thousands of online business owners, is a mental health ambassador, and speaks on stages across the world. Her podcast Think Like a Boss is available via all streaming services.

🌐 www.thinklikeaboss.co

📷 @think_like_a_boss.co

in www.linkedin.com/in/maggie-colette-274620319/

We hope you enjoyed this Hay House book. If you'd like to receive our online catalog featuring additional information on Hay House books and products, or if you'd like to find out more about the Hay Foundation, please contact:

Hay House LLC, P.O. Box 5100, Carlsbad, CA 92018-5100
(760) 431-7695 or (800) 654-5126
www.hayhouse.com® • www.hayfoundation.org

———

Published in Australia by:
Hay House Australia Publishing Pty Ltd
18/36 Ralph St., Alexandria NSW 2015
Phone: +61 (02) 9669 4299
www.hayhouse.com.au

Published in the United Kingdom by:
Hay House UK Ltd
1st Floor, Crawford Corner,
91–93 Baker Street, London W1U 6QQ
Phone: +44 (0)20 3927 7290
www.hayhouse.co.uk

Published in India by:
Hay House Publishers (India) Pvt Ltd
Muskaan Complex, Plot No. 3,
B-2, Vasant Kunj, New Delhi 110 070
Phone: +91 11 41761620
www.hayhouse.co.in

———

Let Your Soul Grow

Experience life-changing transformation—one video at a time—with guidance from the world's leading experts.

www.healyourlifeplus.com

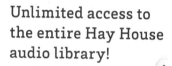

CONNECT WITH
HAY HOUSE
ONLINE

🌐 hayhouse.co.uk	**f** @hayhouse
📷 @hayhouseuk	𝕏 @hayhouseuk
▶ @hayhouseuk	♪ @hayhouseuk

Find out all about our latest books & card decks • Be the first to know about exclusive discounts • Interact with our authors in live broadcasts • Celebrate the cycle of the seasons with us • Watch free videos from your favourite authors • Connect with like-minded souls

'The gateways to wisdom and knowledge are always open.'

Louise Hay